What Must We Teach?

Tim Devlin and Mary Warnock

WHAT MUST WE TEACH?

Temple Smith · London

First published in Great Britain 1977
by Maurice Temple Smith Ltd
37 Great Russell Street, London WC1
© TIM DEVLIN & MARY WARNOCK 1977
ISBN 0 85117 1370 paperback
ISBN 0 85117 1362 cased
Printed in Great Britain by
Billing & Sons Ltd
Guildford, London & Worcester

Education is a quagmire of initials. We have tried to avoid using them as much as possible. The following are used in the book:

AEC	Association of Education Committees
CBI	Confederation of British Industry
CSE	Certificate of Secondary Education
DES	Department of Education and Science
GCE	General Certificate of Education
HMI	Her Majesty's Inspectors
NAS/UWT	National Association of Schoolmasters/Union of Women Teachers
NFER	National Foundation for Educational Research
NUT	National Union of Teachers
OECD	Organization for Economic Co-operation and Development
PE	Physical Education
TES	The Times Educational Supplement
TUC	Trades Union Congress

the Education Minister) and with downright opposition by the National Union of Teachers (NUT), Britain's largest teacher union. Mr Max Morris, one of the most vocal members of the union's executive, called it a 'shoddy public relations gimmick' which was being mounted to divert attention from the Government's cutbacks in the education service and to prepare the way for a sharply interventionist policy in schools.

Four main topics were culled from the prime ministerial speech for special attention at these regional conferences: the idea of a basic or 'common core' curriculum to be taught in all schools; the proper way to assess and monitor standards of performance in education; the training of teachers; and how to improve relations between schools and industry.

The one-day debates were divided so that there was a fifteen-minute address from an invited speaker at the start of each of the four sessions and then an hour to debate each topic. About 200 people were invited by the Department of Education and Science (DES) to get a spread of teachers, industrialists, representatives of parent organisations, trade unionists, educational administrators and academics. The conferences were held at Newcastle upon Tyne, Bradford, Preston, Peterborough, Birmingham, Cardiff, London and Exeter. (The Tory Party and the Scottish Education Department later staged their own conferences.) Shirley Williams chaired the first one and afterwards declared it a great success and suggested that the 'great debate' technique might be used to discuss other such controversial issues as how to educate disadvantaged children and training for 16—19-year-olds. Others were not so certain about the success of the whole exercise. Members of the NUT continued to call it a 'downright farce' and even such a dispassionate and fair-minded critic of the educational scene as John Fairhall of the *Guardian* wrote in his column: 'The Great Debate raises expectations, and to put 200 people into a five-hour debate on the manifold problems of schools, industry and society, can produce nothing more than a skin over the surface, a re-statement of well-known platform positions, and a short canter for a stable of hobby-horses.'

During the early conferences this description was all too true. The second one in Bradford had its moments of high drama when a group of about fifty students demonstrating against the threat of closure of nearby teacher-training colleges broke into Bradford College, where the conference was being held, and threatened to disrupt the proceedings. In the event they satisfied themselves with tapping coins on the windows of the conference hall so that the last hour of the discussion was almost drowned to those within. Such was the standard of debate and the clatter that it was a relief when the hour was over.

Mr Gordon Oakes, the Minister subjected to this outburst of student indignation, returned to the third conference in Preston, where the doors were stoutly guarded by the Lancashire Constabulary, and, learning from the mistakes of the past, bluntly told the participants to throw away their prepared speeches. From then on the standard of the conferences picked up, and with the exception of a fairly disastrous foray into Wales where the debate became bogged down over the lack of Welsh language translation facilities, the conferences moved from strength to strength.

It was never, of course, a 'Great Debate', for people seldom picked up each other's points, but it was a unique exercise in contemplating the country's educational navel. And a very cheap one at that. The eight rounds were costed at £13,050. The main items were £8,100 spent on refreshments including some fine buffet lunches, and £3,850 on publishing documents for use at the conferences including 29,000 copies of the main conference document prepared by the Department — *Educating Our Children: Four Subjects for Debate*. Teacher associations, local education authority organisations, the Trades Union Congress (TUC) and the Confederation of British Industry (CBI), were officially consulted both before and after the regional conferences. At least thirty organisations submitted their views on the topics for debate.

Having collected the results of all these deliberations, the DES set about preparing a final draft after Easter of a Green Paper for further discussion. At this point we put our own pens to paper. The forces of philosophy and journalism joined to produce an alternative version. One of us (Tim Devlin) was the only person to sit through all eight regional conferences, except for one official from the Department. Together or separately we interviewed factory trainers and

11

apprentices in Newcastle, schoolchildren in Yorkshire, teachers in Lancashire, parents in Peterborough and educational administrators in Cardiff. We picked the brains of twenty leading lights in the past and present educational scene, some of whom, quoted by name in the book, have been used as inspiration at the head of each chapter. We have also drawn freely and, inevitably, out of context, from among the 350—400 speeches at the conferences. We apologise in advance to any speakers quoted who are horrified by the conclusions we have come to. We hasten to dissociate ourselves: these views are ours and ours alone.

Some may see the restrictions of the past re-echoed in this book. We do not think they are. The book is based firmly on the future and on the goals expressed by the Prime Minister in his speech: 'To equip children to the best of their ability for a lively, constructive place in society and also to fit them for a job of work. Not one or the other, but both.'

How education can meet *both* these needs is the subject of this book, has been that of the great debates about education in the past and undoubtedly will dominate many of the great debates about education in the future. The Green Paper in July 1977 committed the country to yet another great debate on the curriculum. It called upon teachers and local education authorities to review their curricular practices and to report the results of that review within a year. It thus prolonged the agony of decision-making, before the Government decides what must be the 'core curriculum' that all schools must teach.

But teachers and local authorities should not be the only partners in the education service to be consulted. There is a new partner: the community. The Great Debate of 1976—7 provided the first platform for parents, industrialists, and even a few schoolchildren to discuss what should be taught in schools alongside teachers, academics and educational administrators. If that Great Debate is to mean anything at all, these voices must be heard during the next round of discussions. The Green Paper was published as a consultative document. The new partners in the education service must take part in those further consultations.

1 The Secret Garden

'I believe that the so-called secret garden of the curriculum cannot be allowed to remain so secret after all, and that the key to the door must be found and turned.'

— Mr James Hamilton, Permanent Secretary at the Department of Education and Science, to the annual conference of the Association of Education Committees, 25 June 1976.

To understand the Great Debate and to profit from it, we must recall what led up to it. At the beginning of 1976 Mr Fred Mulley, then Secretary of State for Education and Science, gave the customary New Year address on the state of the nation's education service at the North of England Educational Conference at Lancaster University. He said:

'There is a growing chorus of discontent from parents, teachers and employers about the education provided in a minority of schools, colleges and universities. People are worried about some of the stories about education that make the headlines: William Tyndale, the North London Polytechnic and, not so long ago, troubles at this university itself and indeed many others. The list is too long for comfort.'

What he went on to say was perhaps even more significant: 'Frankly,' he said, 'I have no magic remedies, and I do not believe it is possible to find any.'

It was the first time a government minister had referred to dissatisfaction with the education actually provided in schools. Yet in almost the same breath Mr Mulley had wrung his hands and admitted that he was powerless to do anything

13

about it. How had the voices of discontent grown into a chorus? Why did the man entrusted with the duty of promoting the education service feel so helpless? How had the walls around this 'secret garden' grown up so that what was taught in schools came to be regarded as the preserve of the teaching profession? In the present chapter we shall try to suggest some answers to these questions.

From the end of the Second World War right through the more affluent 1960s British education was in a hopeful, and compared to the present day, very cheerful state. The vast majority of people did not think very much about it. There was a general respect for the teaching profession and a long-established tradition, stemming from the famous public schools, of teachers being *in loco parentis*. Parents were happy with this position and did not resent the notices outside the gates of many schools: 'Parents not allowed beyond this point.'

Those parents who thought very much about education probably recognised the vast strides that had been made in teaching more children, more thoroughly, since the passing of the 1944 Education Act had established free secondary schools for all children. During the late 1950s and early 1960s the talk was of expansion — of training more teachers to teach more children — to meet the needs of the post-war population bulge. The money supply for education seemed endless.

But towards the end of the 1960s mutterings against the education system began to be heard. Looking back ten years later it is possible to see that a time when the organisation of secondary education became a heated party-political issue coincided with a time when Britain's affluence began to run dry and governments had to go back on their commitments to expand the education service.

The phasing out of the 11-plus examination, by which bright children were selected for a more academic education at grammar schools, followed the victory of the Labour Party in the general election of 1964. Its manifesto had contained a commitment to comprehensive secondary schools where all children of all abilities were to be educated under one roof, as happened in the primary schools.

In education the appearance of a Labour Government,

after thirteen years of Tory rule, seemed to signal a general move away from the academic content of education in schools. The publication in 1967 of a report on primary schools of a committee headed by Lady Plowden gave memorable expression and official sanction to a child-centred theory of education. This theory, although not invented by Lady Plowden nor by her committee, was used by the Government as a basis for positive discrimination in favour of primary schools in deprived areas, such as the slum districts of large cities. The areas were called Educational Priority Areas.

The report emphasised the supreme influence of the child's home background during the first five years of life on later performance at school. By recommending positive discrimination in favour of the less well-off children, the report became once and for all associated with a particular kind of politics. Child-centred education was identified with social engineering. The Plowden Report's conclusion, that it was better for children to be taught by finding out for themselves (the discovery method) rather than by having information pumped into them by teachers, seemed so self-evident to all right-thinking liberal people that argument seemed scarcely necessary.

The movement in favour of learning through activity and experience had started to gain ground in Britain with the publication of the Hadow Report, *The Primary School*, in 1931. The curriculum, said Hadow, 'is to be thought of in terms of activity and experience rather than of knowledge to be acquired and facts to be stored. Its aims should be to develop in a child the fundamental human powers and to awaken him to the fundamental interests of civilised life. . . .'

Freedom of children to learn by discovery according to their own development meant also freedom for teachers to interpret the individual needs of children and so control the primary school curriculum. The philosophy of Hadow was put into more definite language by Plowden, but it was given political teeth by the Labour governments of 1964 and 1970. Labour Ministers hastened the trend towards the large-scale phasing out of the 11-plus examination which was the last formal external constraint on primary school teaching.

Because it was political it became controversial. Just as the

15

British primary school and its informal 'open' education were being most ardently admired and imitated in the United States, the growing doubters on the right of the political spectrum emerged in this country. Were the children who were supposed to grow and flourish at school, and above all actually to *enjoy* their school life, learning enough? Was the abolition of the 11-plus examination simply a way of ensuring that their deficiences would not be immediately revealed?

These fears were expressed in 1969 in the first *Black Paper*, a collection of essays (edited by C. B. Cox and A. E. Dyson, published by the Critical Quarterly Society) which often used language so immoderate and grossly lacking in balance as to undermine the credibility of even manifestly true statements. But it did issue the following long-overdue warning:

> 'There is a great danger that the traditional high standards of English education are being overthrown. At primary school some teachers are taking to extremes the belief that children must not be told anything but must find out for themselves. At the post-11 stage there is a strong impetus to abolish streaming, and the grammar school concepts of discipline and hard work are treated with contempt.'

The first *Black Paper* was greeted with derision by educationists. Further *Black Papers* followed. In the later ones a moving spirit was Dr Rhodes Boyson, a former comprehensive school supporter, headmaster of Highbury Grove School, Islington, London, an engaging publicity-seeker, who became Conservative MP for Brent North in 1974 and junior Opposition spokesman on education at the end of 1976. The *Black Paper* might have been consigned to oblivion had it not been for the unfortunate intervention of Mr Edward Short, then Secretary of State for Education and Science. In a speech in the House of Commons he greeted its publication as 'the blackest day in education history for 100 years'. He thus ensured the widespread publicity given to its views and the eventual success of *Black Papers* two, three, four and five.

From then on stories of widespread indiscipline, violence, and vandalism in schools were given full coverage in the press. They were supported by some of the teaching profession, first by the National Association of Schoolmasters which, by referenda of its members, lent the stories some statistical basis, then by less militant unions such as the Assistant Masters' Association and by the National Association of Head Teachers and finally even by some of the branches of the National Union of Teachers, whose executive had always maintained that the reports were much exaggerated.

Teachers blamed the increasing indiscipline on lack of support from local education authorities, on apathetic parents and on the permissive society. But the tables seemed to be turned on them when the industrialists joined in the act. Theirs was a two-pronged attack: first they complained about products of the school system — recruits to their firms who could not read nor write. And their criticisms were not just confined to 16-year-old craft apprentices but applied also to 22-year-old university graduates. Secondly they complained that teachers were cut off from industry, disliked industry, and promoted that dislike among their pupils. One of the first industrial salvoes against the teachers was fired by Sir Arnold Weinstock, managing director of the General Electric Company, and one of Britain's leading industrialists. In an article headed 'I blame the teachers' he wrote in *The Times Educational Supplement* (23 January 1976):

'From the outside the education system does not appear to be run with model efficiency. There are more people employed in education in non-teaching posts than in actual teaching. Second, the teaching profession, like some others, has made its members unsackable except for gross misconduct.

'Human nature being what it is, such a condition of feather-bedding sooner or later increases to the limit the number of bad-but-not-rotten apples in the barrel. This raises the whole thorny question of accountability of teachers and educationists to the community.'

Later he wrote: 'Teachers fulfil an essential function in the community but, having themselves chosen not to go into industry, they often deliberately or more usually uncon-sciously instil in their pupils a similar bias. In so doing they are not serving the democratic will.' In this way were teachers blamed for Britain's economic ills. Sir Arnold conceded that

17

industry itself could put its house in order and make itself more attractive to schoolchildren. But the idea of the teacher as a scapegoat had been established.

Many parent voices too added to the disquiet that standards of performance in schools were declining. There were obvious reasons why this could be so. Between 1966 and 1976 the number of primary school teachers increased by a third and of secondary school teachers by more than a half. Some, who undoubtedly should never have gone into teaching, drifted into it in response to a government campaign to get more recruits into the profession because of the rising birth-rate.

The number of parents deciding to send their children to recognised independent schools rose, despite the soaring costs of school fees. They were encouraged by tales of crumbling standards in state schools, the recounting of which grew into an industry in itself and will be discussed more fully in another chapter. A survey by the National Foundation for Educational Research (NFER) in 1972 first gave firm dispassionate evidence that standards of literacy had dropped. Later, on no really firm statistical basis, the country was shocked to learn in 1973 that there were one million illiterate adults. That number was then doubled and no one disputed it. At a time when many teachers were fleeing from particularly difficult jobs teaching particularly difficult children in particularly difficult schools, there were reliable reports that up to one third of school leavers were departing from some large London schools functionally illiterate and innumerate.

Then in 1975 an event hit the headlines which encap-sulated all these anxieties and brought them to a head. The troubles at William Tyndale junior school, Islington, to which Mr Mulley referred in his speech quoted at the beginning of this chapter, were flashed across the television screens to a nation bewildered about what was actually going on in schools, confused enough and credulous enough to believe anything.

This was an affair at a small inner London junior school (for children aged seven to eleven) where there had been a complete breakdown in the relationships between most of the teachers, on the one hand, and the school's managing

18

body and some parents of children at the school on the other. In less than two years the school roll had dropped from 250 to less than 150, far more rapidly and drastically than any other school in the area. The managers accused the teachers of being politically motivated and of having gone overboard for 'progressive' methods of teaching. The teachers accused the managers of stirring up trouble and banned them from visiting the school during school hours. The headmaster shocked some parents by saying that the typewriter had made writing skills unnecessary. There were complaints that children were left to watch television and play table-tennis for long periods.

One teacher who was supposed to be teaching reading to a group of children of different ages was alleged to have written up on the blackboard: 'I hate reading groups'! and to have sent the children out to play. Anecdotes of this kind abounded and the Press and the media generally made a meal out of them. What made matters worse was that during a detailed inquiry into affairs at the school held by the Inner London Education Authority over nearly seventy days in 1975–6, it emerged that although officials of the authority knew what was going on, they seemed powerless to intervene. Indeed, after the 250,000-word report by Mr Robin Auld, QC, who carried out the inquiry, was published, Sir Ashley Bramall, leader of the education authority, admitted that the authority had perhaps forgotten that it had powers under the 1944 Education Act to intervene. It would have to reconsider its policy of delegating all control over schools to the head teachers.

What the Auld Report actually said was not as important as the general impact of the whole prolonged affair. The teachers involved went on strike for three weeks in September 1975 and set up an alternative school in a nearby chapel. For this action a special disciplinary tribunal recommended in April 1977 that they be dismissed. The William Tyndale incidents seemed to confirm everyone's worst fears. The community in the form of managers and parents had been totally disregarded by the teachers, who, in pursuit of their own educational and political ideals, seemed to regard themselves as obliged to no authority and account-able in no way to the public. In fact Auld judiciously apportioned blame to all parties in the dispute — but that was not the way it looked, even though the chairman of the education authority and some of the managers felt obliged to resign.

The Government was already beginning to show that it could not remain on the sidelines and must do something about the growing concern and alarm. In 1975 it had set up a committee of inquiry into the management and government of schools, under the chairmanship of Tom Taylor, former leader of Blackburn Council. It also, that year, announced a shift in the purpose of the Assessment of Performance Unit, a one-man operation within the DES which was signposted in 1974 as a measure to help disadvantaged and under-achieving children. It was now going to monitor standards of numeracy and literacy among all schoolchildren.

Mr Sam Fisher, chairman of the NUT's education committee, was one of the first to grasp the significance of the Government's move. He warned his union's annual conference in April 1975: 'There are indeed signs that the department has an interest in the curriculum in the recent announcement [about the unit].... We are looking at it very closely. There could be serious dangers in some of the Minister's proposals.'

From the point of view of Britain's largest teaching union much worse was to come. A report by an international body, the Organization for Economic Co-operation and Development (OECD) had in May 1975 criticised the way planning was carried out by the DES. We will return to the OECD report at the end of this chapter but it was very much the fuse that sparked off the Great Debate because it led to a parliamentary watchdog committee deciding to look for itself at priorities and decision-making in the Department.

The 1944 Education Act gave the Minister of Education (later Secretary of State for Education and Science) the responsibility of 'promoting' the education of the people. But nowhere in that or subsequent Acts was he given any responsibility over the curriculum in schools. The joke put out by Mr George Tomlinson, Education Minister in the post-war Labour Government, was that 'Minister knew nowt about curriculum'. By the end of the 1960s this joke had become a reality and one regarded with all seriousness by the NUT leadership. Not only were ministers afraid to

20

intervene, but their departments found it more convenient to shelter behind the catch-phrase that 'Ministers did not intervene in matters of school curriculum'. The group of MPs (Education, Arts and Home Office Subcommittee of the Expenditure Committee) sitting at the end of 1975 was told that if all the schools in the land stopped teaching mathematics, the Secretary of State for Education and Science could according to law stand up in the House of Commons and say: 'That has nothing to do with me.'

This was the apparent constitutional position of powerlessness from which Mr Mulley spoke at the beginning of 1976 when he said there were 'no magic remedies'. During the year there were three important changes of *dramatis personae*: there was a new Prime Minister; there was Mrs Shirley Williams, a new dynamic Secretary of State for Education and Science, always late for meetings and full of apologies and energy, and there was a new Permanent Secretary — Mr James Hamilton.

Mr Hamilton struck the first note of change. Something of a whizz-kid from the boffin rooms of aircraft research, Mr Hamilton had become deputy secretary of the Cabinet Office. Rather ominously for education he had, between 1966 and 1970, been director general of the Concorde project at the Ministry of Technology. A new broom, and a Scottish one, had swept into the Department.

He did not lose much time, He took the occasion of his first public engagement (the annual general meeting of the Association of Education Committees in June) to give a broad hint that the Department was preparing to intervene in the 'secret garden of the curriculum'. The relevant part of his speech is used as the heading to this chapter. It marked a crucial turning-point. Against the customary tradition of reticence, a civil servant had grasped the initiative.

Mr Callaghan, who succeeded Harold Wilson as Prime Minister in April, was also preparing a major speech on education for reasons which will be discussed more fully in Chapter 3. He asked the DES to prepare him a briefing memorandum for it. This secret memorandum was leaked to the *Guardian* in September and became known as the *Yellow Book* or *Yellow Paper* because of the colour of its rather graphic cover. It was not very complimentary about the

21

country's teachers. It said that some primary school teachers had allowed performance in the basic skills of reading, writing and arithmetic to suffer as a result of an 'uncritical application' of informal methods. The time was almost certainly ripe for a corrective shift of emphasis. The *Yellow Paper* criticised the inadequacy of the teaching of numeracy and literacy in secondary schools. It complained that children were being allowed to choose unbalanced, or at least unprofitable, courses and that not enough of them for the country's needs were choosing to study scientific and technological subjects. The paper criticised the teaching force for not being equipped 'as we would wish' to teach certain subjects (mathematics and modern languages particularly) and in general, less precise, terms it complained: 'In an almost desperate attempt to modify styles of teaching and learning so as to capture the imagination and enlist the co-operation of their most difficult pupils, some of them have possibly been too ready to drop their sights in setting standards of performance and have failed to develop new styles of assessment.'

This, then, was the briefing paper before the Prime Minister's famous speech and before the Great Debate was launched. It will be useful to sum up what the main anxieties were in the minds of parents, employers, society at large, and civil servants at the DES. They seem to be three in number. First, there was the fear that education in general had become out of touch with what was actually demanded of it in the real world. It neither prepared children for employment nor ensured their academic competence. Second, there was a distrust of child-centred 'progressive' methods of teaching shared by the leaders of the two main political parties; and third, in a way embracing both these fears, and more important than either by itself, was the growing alarm that teachers had complete control over what was taught in schools. Indeed their power had become so great that no one could intervene to question it.

To what extent was this last fear justified? We must look briefly at the actual position of teachers in the hierarchy of educational power and how they came to be in the position they are now in.

It is not always remembered that the freedom which all

British schools have from a prescribed curriculum laid down by central government is only thirty-three years old. There was a time when what teachers taught was more firmly prescribed by central government in Britain than almost anywhere else in the world. In order to present the teachers' case fairly we must go back more than 100 years to a notorious system known as 'payment by results'.

At that time the education system was run by a special committee of the Privy Council and most schools were paid for out of grants from this committee. The Revised Code of 1862 set these grants at eight shillings a year per child who attended school more than 200 times. But the code fixed yearly tests in reading, writing and arithmetic and deducted 2s 8d from the grant for each test a child failed. The teachers' positions and the future of the school itself were therefore dependent on the results of these tests.

John Adamson in his *A Short History of Education* (Cambridge University Press, 1919) wrote: 'The Revised Code encouraged the neglect of the intelligent and the reduction of all pupils to the level of the lowest capacity in a given school, or class.' He said it rewarded 'cramming' and stereotyped the 'false idea' that the three Rs were the all-important rudiments of education, diverting attention from the moral function of the school and exercise in manual skills.

The 'payment by results' system was abolished by 1895 but its effects lived on as many teachers were so conditioned to cramming their children that they continued doing so. It is a bogey to which leaders of teacher unions often refer when discussing a national system of monitoring and assessing performances in schools. When we interviewed Sir Ronald Gould, a former general secretary of the NUT, he referred to a quotation from Matthew Arnold, the nineteenth-century poet who also belonged to the corps of Her Majesty's Inspectorate. Arnold had warned that no system of national monitoring could be established except by 'payment for results'. It would lead to teachers teaching for examinations and ignoring everything else, he had said.

The freedom from central control which teachers cherish was a long time coming. The first steps were taken in 1906 when the then Board of Education made it clear that teachers were to be relied upon, in the questions of methods and of curriculum, to set their own standards. They were to be made aware of their own independence. In a famous foreword to the first *Handbook of Suggestions* from His Majesty's Inspectorate, Sir Robert Morant, the Board's Permanent Secretary, wrote: 'The only uniformity that the Board of Education desire to see in the teaching of public elementary schools is that the teacher should think for himself and work out for himself such methods of teaching as may use his powers to best advantage and be best suited to the particular needs and conditions of the school.' Professor Harold Dent, the educational historian, commented: 'I venture to think that Morant . . . gave to the public elementary school an inspiring ideal at which to aim, and to its teachers a professional freedom without precedent in England or in any other country' (*1870–1970, A Century of Growth in English Education*, Longmans, 1970).

The official policy or 'suggestions' laid down by Morant when he reorganised the school curriculum in 1904 was that elementary schools should normally teach English language, handwriting, arithmetic, drawing, practical handicraft, gardening, domestic and other subjects, nature study, geography, history, singing, hygiene, physical training, and morals.

However, far greater freedom was to come. The regulations for elementary schools were radically changed by the 1926 code which simply stated: 'The secular instruction in a school . . . must be in accordance with a suitable curriculum and syllabus framed with due regard to the organisation and circumstances of the school concerned'. Curriculum regulations in the secondary schools to which only a minority of pupils proceeded at the age of eleven remained for nearly twenty years more.

It has recently been suggested that the motive for the freeing of the elementary schools may have been political. Lord Eustace Percy was President of the Board of Education at the time and he may have wanted to remove control of the curriculum in elementary schools from the hands of politicians because of the danger of a majority socialist government winning power. By leaving secondary schools under restrictions and freeing elementary schools, he may have wanted to drive a wedge between them to make it less easy to introduce a scheme of secondary education for all children. At that time many Conservatives feared the consequences of the working classes being 'over-educated'. (See John White, *The Curriculum*, Doris Lee Lectures, 1975, University of London Institute of Education.)

Restrictions for secondary schools were not lifted until the 1944 Education Act. The last prescribed syllabus dates back to the grant regulations for secondary schools in 1933 which state: 'Adequate provision must be made for instruction in English language and literature, at least one language other than English, geography, history, mathematics, science, drawing, singing, manual instruction in the case of boys, domestic science in the case of girls, physical exercises and for organised games'. The 1944 Education Act which replaced this laid down: 'The Local Education Authority shall determine the general educational character of the school and its place in the local education system. Subject thereto the governors shall have the general direction of the conduct of the curriculum.'

Officially, this is the situation today. But in practice the governors or managers of a school exert little influence on the curriculum. The 1944 Act laid down the ideal that children should be taught according to their age, abilities and aptitudes. It gave teachers considerable freedom to teach what they liked and according to the methods they preferred. But they operated in the 1950s within certain constraints.

For one thing curriculum in schools was and is very much determined by text-books, many of which once chosen are slavishly followed. But unlike other countries, text-books in Britain are not prescribed by central government. Teachers can choose which text-books they want to use. If they do not like any on the market, they can, and many do, use their own work materials. So that text-books in this country are further weapons which ensure the hold of the teachers on the education system.

A second constraint was provided by public examinations in the control of examination boards which were largely university-dominated. Then there were constraints placed upon them by external decisions made by the local authority, subject sometimes to central government approval,

25

with regard to type of building, resources, number of teachers, salary structures and so on. The actual organisation of the schools again imposed restrictions — whether or not a school was comprehensive, whether it did, or did not, have a sixth form, for example. Finally and pervasively, there was the influence of the head teacher.

Heads of schools select staff (with or without help from the governors). They determine how the school is to be governed, how decisions are taken, how many staff meetings are held, and so on. They strongly influence the size of the different departments. They are to a large degree responsible for the allocation of resources as between science and arts subjects and they influence, for example, whether the school concentrates on music or sports.

However, teachers and head teachers together formed a strong partnership as the professional associations to which many of them jointly belonged became more militant throughout the 1960s and in the early 1970s. And so Mrs Shirley Williams could plausibly say during an Open University television programme in March 1977 that teachers' organisations had eroded the power of local authorities and central government in the last ten years. The head (and assistant teachers where they were consulted) provided the greatest single influence on individual school curricula. She said this contrasted with the legal framework in which local authorities via school governors and managers supposedly had control.

Moreover, first the National Association of Schoolmasters and then the NUT, the two biggest teacher unions, had become affiliated to the TUC. The growth of teacher professionalism was a factor that had increasingly to be taken into account in post-war curriculum decisions. And now, with the might of the trade union movement behind it, the NUT is jealously preparing to protect its freedom.

The head teachers and teachers have also extended their control into the examination system. The Beloe Report of 1960 recommended a new examination, slightly below the ordinary level (O Level) of the General Certificate of Education (GCE) and designed for the secondary modern pupil. The Certificate of Secondary Education (CSE) was introduced in 1964 and organised on a regional basis.

Teachers established control over the regional committees and decided their own curricula for a wide range of subjects. In the case of Mode 3 — one of the three forms of examination in the system — teachers within a school not only design the syllabus but set the examinations and mark their own pupils' work. The school, subject to monitoring of a random sample by the examination board, thus becomes virtually autonomous, like a university awarding its own degrees.

The peak of teachers' freedom came in 1970 with the plan to merge the two examinations at 16-plus (GCE O level and CSE) into a common system which looked as if it would extend teacher control because the Mode 3 form was recommended for much of the proposed examination. Just as the Great Debate got under way, this plan was held up by the Government for further consideration.

Other influences which might be thought to curb the teachers' freedom are those of the local authority advisers and of the national corps of Her Majesty's Inspectors (HMIs). But the local advisers, organisers and inspectors, as they are variously called, are more concerned with administrative matters than with inspecting what is actually being taught in schools. The HMIs too rarely use their official inspectorial function. The *Handbook of Suggestions* which they issued to teachers every year faded out after 1937.

An attempt to intervene in the curriculum was made by Sir David (now Lord) Eccles, Minister of Education, in 1962. He has been credited with coining the famous phrase 'secret garden of the curriculum'. He told us that he first used it, to the consternation of the Senior Chief Inspector ('a nervous man'), when suggesting an attempt to introduce modern mathematics teaching.

Sir David set up a 'Curriculum Study Group' within his Ministry. This was replaced by the Schools Council, an advisory body on curriculum and examinations, in 1964. The council was dominated by teachers, representatives of the teaching unions, and took away many of the functions that Sir David had hoped would have been given to the inspectorate. It is difficult to determine why the inspectorate was further weakened.

Lord Eccles told us in January 1977: 'I wanted the HMIs

taken out of the building and made into a think-tank, a research and development unit, to help the Minister. I do not know of any big industry that can get on without an R and D department.' He recalled that his group failed principally because the inspectors themselves were not enthusiastic. ('They had too much liking for being big people when they went round schools'.) Lord Boyle, who as Sir Edward Boyle succeeded Sir David in 1962, also told us he did not remember the curriculum study group being defeated by teacher opposition. He said: 'There was a general agreement with the teacher associations that we should bring the partners in on the curriculum study group instead of it just being the cutting edge of the inspectorate – a term used by Sir Toby Weaver, former deputy secretary at the DES. The idea was to bring in the teacher associations, the local authority associations, and teachers in independent as well as maintained schools.'

Lord Alexander, secretary of the old Association of Education Committees and the most effective of the teachers' employers, and Sir Ronald Gould both told us that Eccles's plan was dropped after they had opposed it strongly. Professor Maurice Kogan, professor of government and social administration at Brunel University, said the Schools Council resulted from teacher objections to the creation of the study group. (*Educational Policy Making*, George Allen & Unwin, 1975.) This is the general view held today.

Jenkins and Shipman in their book, *Curriculum: an introduction* (Open Books, 1976) put the matter this way: 'The Ministry, through the Curriculum Study Group, seemed to be threatening central control over the curriculum which had seemed to be firmly in the hands of teachers. The study group was abandoned after union pressure in 1963, and the Schools Council was established with a complicated set of checks and balances to ensure that the teacher unions have a majority whenever educational policy is being decided.'

The Council's governing body has about eighty members and it is a constitutional requirement that the teacher unions should have a built-in majority. The unions also have a majority on all the Council's committees except its finance committee. Maurice Kogan, who spent fourteen years in the DES, where he was a Private Secretary to Sir Edward Boyle, called the council 'undoubtedly a triumph of the established teacher associations'.

A good deal of the responsibility for that 'teacher triumph' must be laid at the door of the Department, for unless the Department had been weak, the teachers could not have become so strong. If the Department had made clear decisions and had let these be known, there could never have been such a universal feeling that children at school were being swept along on an uncontrollable tide of educational dogma and ideological enthusiasm.

The *Yellow Paper* (the DES memorandum referred to above) was presumably written by the inspectorate in part because it contains some smug but revealing remarks about itself: 'HM Inspectorate is without doubt the most powerful single agency to influence what goes on in schools, both in kind and standard.' This led Sir Alex Smith, chairman of the Schools Council, to argue, with it seems to us impeccable logic, that if the weaknesses in the schools, which the secret memorandum described, did indeed exist, then if the inspectorate was really the most powerful agency for the improvement of schools, it was the inspectors who above all should be blamed. And blamed they often were during the course of the Great Debate for any mess that Britain's education service was in.

Mrs E. Diamond, a Tyneside councillor, said at the first regional conference in Newcastle upon Tyne that inspectors had advised teachers not to bother to teach children to read because they were bound to be attracted by all the lovely books in the library anyway. Mr C. Pollard, a junior school headmaster, told the conference in Birmingham: 'We have suffered from HMIs who have come into schools and suggested that this subject should be taken, and that subject should be taken, so that children have been deprived of basic numeracy and literacy.' Mr Hywel Thomas, of the National Association of Schoolmasters/Union of Women Teachers (NAS/UWT), also blamed the inspectors for being largely responsible for declining standards. He told the conference in Cardiff: 'For the past decade we have had people going into our schools, passing to us half-baked and barely understood ideas. Many of the younger teachers found it very difficult to challenge them.'

29

The Department as a whole has combined feebleness in the analysis of where power actually resides in curriculum matters with an obsessive secrecy about what its policies actually are. We shall return to the proper role of the DES later, but the OECD report was most critical about this aspect. It summarised the Department's own views as follows:

The feeling exists strongly that when it comes to planning leading to policy decisions for which resources have to be secured and allocated . . . informal methods [of consultation] utilised by sensitive and fair-minded government civil-servants are superior to highly structured formal procedures which invite half-baked and politically sectarian opinions, and encourage demagogy, confrontation and publicity battles, leading to a lot of waste of time.

The report then comments on this attitude:

This feeling may be well-grounded but the fact remains that the United Kingdom offers an example of educational planning in which the structure for ensuring public participation are limited. This has at least two consequences. One is that in certain cases policy is less likely to be understood, and therefore less likely to be whole-heartedly accepted, when the processes which lead up to its formation are guarded as arcane secrets. The second is that goals and priorities, once established, may go on being taken for granted and hence escape the regular scrutiny which may be necessary for an appropriate re-alignment of policy.

A leading article in *The Times Higher Education Supplement* (9 May 1975) sums up the report as really saying that British education is administered by a 'brilliant and professional but cloistered elite which curbs its political masters, is subject to no parliamentary scrutiny, controls the education service while affecting to follow the consensus, dislikes open planning and participation and is defensive of its powers'.

In defence of the Department it could be said that its secrecy and evasiveness arise out of weakness rather than out of a Machiavellian cunning or a lust for power. It has become slightly more open in its publication of documents since

Shirley Williams became Secretary of State, but the fact remains that it has allowed the teachers to take over responsibility for promoting the education of the people as far as schoolchildren are concerned. It is a myth that the DES cannot intervene in curriculum matters generally, for it does control curriculum in the colleges of further education, as Mr Gerald Fowler, a former Minister of State at the Department, has pointed out (in *Curriculum Innovation*, edited by Alan Harris *et al.*, an Open University set book, 1975). It does approve courses for certificates and diplomas. Its inspectors have no inhibitions about rejecting courses and are responsible for syllabuses to such an extent that Dr George Brosan, director of North East London Polytechnic, has complained: 'The staff in the colleges, with a great deal of enthusiasm and efficiency, operate a system that has been designed by some outside body . . . the great majority of teachers in the public sector of further and higher education are compelled, despite their abilities, to perform the function of technicians.' (G. Brosan *et al*, *Patterns and Politics in Higher Education*, Penguin, 1971.)

If the Department plays with its cards close to its chest, if it sometimes seems to have no views at all on the most important questions, this may be because it quite genuinely believes that its eroded powers can best be preserved by quietness and passivity. This situation cannot be allowed to go on. Its position in the order of things must be clarified. The period after the Great Debate and the publication of the Green Paper is the appropriate time for this.

Since the NUT has become a vocal part of the TUC, it can be expected that this clarification will be painful. But the intervention of the Prime Minister at Ruskin College has shattered the myth that central government cannot intervene in curriculum matters. Control is exercised indirectly through its distribution of teachers and resources; it is exercised directly in the realm of further education. This will become more important as more links are developed between colleges of further education and sixth forms in schools. The DES, teachers' unions, and local education authorities will sooner or later have to redefine their spheres of influence.

Now is the time. The Prime Minister's speech is not the only catalyst. It took advantage of a general feeling, within many educational circles and outside, that things could not go on as they were and a clash between the main teachers' union and the Government was inevitable. The educational ferment concerns the examinations. The system of 16-plus examinations is up for grabs. The Schools Council has been twiced rebuffed in its attempts to reorganise examinations. It has been rubbed home that just as it cannot tell teachers what to do, it can only advise the Government. First when Mrs Margaret Thatcher turned down the proposal for a 20-point grading scheme for A Level in 1972, and second with the decision to re-examine its plans for O Level and CSE, the Government has reflected a general feeling that the teaching unions can no longer be trusted with the exclusive charge of the country's children. The Schools Council has itself recognised this and is reviewing its constitution to see if it can bring in more members from the community.

Local government reorganisation in 1974 coincided with a time of extreme financial stringency. Each department has to fight for its own funding. Education has been subject perhaps to disproportionate cuts. Direct central government funding of specific educational programmes is now very likely. Shirley Williams has already hinted that this is the way she will promote the training of teachers who are in service. This opens a whole new area of central government intervention. It is just another indication that changes, with or without the Great Debate, are in the air.

2 Foreign Comparisons

'We do not want a common system like other countries.
The British system can be proud of its freedom of education.
It is unique and one of the best systems in the world.'
— Dr Trevor Jones, principal adviser for South Glamorgan
education authority, *The Times*, 22 March 1977.

Before deciding on any changes in the English and Welsh
system, it is important to look at the way education is
developing on the Continent and elsewhere. The main
elements of a country's education system are deeply rooted
in its traditions, culture, its whole way of life, which have
evolved over the years. There are bound to be inherent
differences between countries. But there are also likely to
be common trends which will affect the way our systems
evolve in the future.

The declining birth-rate (the pill-drop, as the West
Germans call it) is affecting all our education systems and
has made us look at the structure of our schools and the
size of the teaching force. The economic recession has made
us concentrate on priorities and try to cut out unnecessary
overlap. Unemployment, and teenage unemployment in
particular, is becoming a permanent ugly fact of life as a
result of increased mechanisation. Hundreds of thousands of
teenagers who are leaving our schools unqualified have little
hope of finding satisfactory employment. Rapidly changing
technologies are making skills swiftly redundant and creating
the need for new ones, and so on.

Membership, too, of an enlarged European Community is
beginning to make England more conscious of educational

practice in other member countries. The basic principles of educational collaboration in the Community are being agreed which, if they lead to nothing else, could lead to a reduction of needless differences so that students can move more easily between schools and colleges in member countries.

There are three distinct models on which Western European education systems are based: the Scandinavian, the French and the West German. The curriculum in Scandinavia, which includes Finland as well as Sweden and Norway (Denmark in many respects is a law unto herself), is seen as an essential part of a wider social reform. It has been one of the main agents whereby the Swedes, for example, have striven since the War to bring about an equal and classless society. The education system is therefore a highly bureaucratised model. The National Board of Education in Sweden publishes the *Läroplan*, a detailed curriculum brief which is binding on teachers. Curriculum documents, in which teachers have little part, are the main means of bringing about curriculum changes.

The second model, the French, is again highly centralised and is used in countries such as Belgium, Austria, Spain and Italy. In France the Minister of Education has overall control of the curriculum but, unlike the Scandinavian model, there is a fair amount of delegation downwards. National curriculum guidelines are drafted by a series of curriculum commissions on which teachers are represented. There is a strong tradition of endless consultations with teacher associations and national parent organisations before any reform is decided upon. But once guidelines or reforms are passed a highly trained corps of inspectors makes sure that they are adhered to. Teachers are civil servants. Detailed *dossiers* are kept on all children and passed on to the schools they move to.

The West German system is completely decentralised in that the eleven *Länder* are the main controllers of the curriculum. A conference of Education Ministers from each *Land* tries to ensure conformity of syllabuses throughout the country but there is a fierce suspicion of any central government interference. A great deal of respect is accorded to academic research and universities are the main curriculum development agencies.

34

In the United States, Canada and Australia, syllabuses are laid down by school boards. But Britain belongs to no group. She is the only country in the developed Western World where schools do not have to conform to a prescribed common syllabus laid down from outside. In England and Wales the legal responsibility for the curriculum has been given to 104 local education authorities. They in turn have delegated it to the governing and managing bodies of each school. In practice, as mentioned in Chapter 1, the governors' influence on the curriculum is limited. The head teacher, as the saying goes, is 'Captain of the Ship'. The only statutory requirement is a religious assembly in the morning and an unspecified period of religious education to be given each week, which according to a survey by the Assistant Masters Association is flouted by five secondary schools out of six.

The differences between schools cause confusion for pupils who move from one school to another and from one stage of education to another. This was a particular cause of concern during the Great Debate. At the first of the eight regional conferences Mr B. J. Jarvis, representing the food, drink and tobacco training board, said that junior managers who moved with their jobs from Newcastle to Norwich to Buckinghamshire were at a considerable disadvantage because they could not find schools to which it was easy for their children to move. He said with some exasperation: 'The assumption that there should be a lack of a common core curriculum is one of the heaven-sent commandments of British education.'

Education in other countries is more suited to the increasing mobility of family life. At one extreme, pupils at French schools in the Lebanon can pick up their education where they left off in Paris or at the London Lycée. At the other, pupils at Risedale secondary school near Richmond, Yorkshire, which has 200 children from army families at Catterick camp moving into it and about 200 others moving out of it each year, has a timetable which has much more in common with British army schools in West Germany than with another school serving mainly army families in Corsham, Wiltshire. The first has a traditional timetable of separate subjects, the second operates an 'integrated' school day with groups of subjects being combined. The one

35

does the old mathematics, the other does the new. Sweden, France and Scotland have all embraced the new mathematics. The Irish Republic blends the two. But England is a chequer-board of old and new.

How does central control affect teaching and teaching methods? The freedom of the English education system has been contrasted with the apparent servitude of those on the Continent. The Great Debate was conducted in England against a foreign backdrop of the French education minister lurking in the wings, looking at his watch and declaring with conviction which particular textbook each particular grade of pupils was studying at that hour on a Monday morning. It is a parody which is still believed even by some people high up in the education service in England. For example, Mr Gordon Oakes, Minister of State with responsibility for higher education, when he wound up the last regional conference at Exeter on 28 March 1977 made it clear that 'the cry from the conferences has not been for a Continental system where every child reads the same book at the same time'.

It is doubtful if this description was ever true, even when another Great British Bogey, the Emperor Napoleon, was stalking the battlefields of Europe. No country in the West has had much success in controlling exactly what teachers teach in the classroom and how they teach it. Teaching is an individual human interchange between teachers and children. It could be argued that teachers are freer when prescribed syllabuses are set by a remote central influence than they are when the head teacher or head of department, who is on the spot, is responsible.

However, what the other Western education systems appear to do is to set out norms or guidelines as to how much time should be devoted per week to each listed subject. A limited choice of textbooks is prescribed and schools which do not make their own work-sheets and other materials are heavily dependent on educational publishers, often working to government specifications. The syllabuses prescribed for French schools, although they have become more informal since the student troubles of 1968, do lay down a certain number of hours per week for subjects even in primary schools. Thus the syllabus for the *cours élémentaire* and *cours moyen* for the last four years or so of primary school lays down fifteen hours of basic subjects (French ten hours, arithmetic five hours), six hours of what can be broadly described as 'aware-making' subjects (history, geography, natural sciences, moral and civic instruction, art and music) and six hours for physical training and sport.

A document produced in 1976 by President Giscard D'Estaing's government is also trying, against heavy teacher union opposition, to prepare the way for unstreamed comprehensive education during the first cycle of French secondary education from about the age of 11 to the age of 14 or 15. The 27-hour weekly timetable is to be divided as follows: French, 6 hours; mathematics, 4 hours; modern languages, 4 hours; science, 3 hours; history and geography, 3 hours; manual and technician education, 2 hours; art and music, 2 hours; physical training, 3 hours.

A common core curriculum is extended into the latter stages of secondary school: French, history, geography, civics, one modern language, mathematics, physics and physical training. Not only are the French inspectors still among the most traditional in Europe, but central government has recently introduced a mechanism for supporting services from the centre downwards. In 1968 it set up an official body — Institut National de Recherche et de Documentation Pédagogiques (the INRDP) — to co-ordinate curriculum and research, and a thoroughly efficient-looking network of pedagogic centres which undertake both the dissemination of new findings and teaching methods and the training of teachers.

In West Germany new reforms in the pattern of studies for the top end of secondary schools came into force in September 1976. They included 10–12 hours a week of compulsory subjects — German, a foreign language, mathematics or a science.

Guidelines for secondary schools in Italy (there are none for primary schools) specify the following broad fields of interest: Italian and one modern language; aesthetic awareness of art, architecture, literature and music; history, mathematics, logic, civics and moral and religious education.

The subjects covered are probably the same and in the same quantity as in many schools in Britain. The French spend more time on the native language, and the West Germans spend more time on foreign languages (usually English) than the British. Otherwise the main difference is whether or not the curriculum is positively laid down for schools.

Even in this respect the Continental system is becoming increasingly flexible to allow degrees of participation by parents, pupils and teachers. Councils of parents to take a part in the running of schools are being encouraged in Scotland, France, Italy and Denmark. In Denmark pupils were allowed for the first time in 1977 to decide whether they wanted to proceed from the lower secondary school to the upper secondary school at the age of sixteen. Previously they had been selected by their teachers. In Sweden each school used to have a detailed curriculum issued by the National Board of Education specifying the time to be devoted to each subject and the topics to be covered. These mandatory syllabuses are now more and more being presented as guidelines, and schools are being allowed to group subjects. A certain amount of decentralisation of the system is happening in both Sweden and Norway under which experimental work is being carried out by teams in schools supported by universities and colleges of education.

Teachers, after years of reliance on registered textbooks and other regulations (one Swedish school is reported to have rung up the National Education Board in 1973 when the king died to ask it if it should fly the flag) find it difficult to take the initiative. In 1973 the French Government passed a law giving teachers one tenth of the timetable to use as they wished. The trouble is that many teachers do not know what to do with it. An OECD *Handbook on Curriculum Development* (published 1975) commenting on the French education system said: 'The average classroom teacher, although in theory free to develop his own approach within the framework provided by the national curricular guide-lines, is usually content to accept the pattern worked out in one of the standard textbooks.'

An OECD report on the West German education system in 1972 criticised it for being too slow to change and recommended that schools should have more autonomy. In 1973 the *Bildunsgrat* (German Education Council) recom-

38

mended that there should be more participation by pupils, parents and teachers. Herr Hans Brugelmann and Clive Hopes in their paper presented to the Fifth Annual Conference of the British Educational Administration Society in London (September 1976) said: 'The problem is that under the traditional system the teachers have not had enough preparation to be more inquiring and they have not been expected to participate.' Because of the way school hours are arranged in West Germany (generally 8 a.m. to lunchtime) teachers hardly have time to meet each other or to work in teams, but they do have considerable freedom. Brugelmann and Hopes said: 'Teachers have considerable individual freedom in developing their own curricula from the outlines laid down in the curriculum frameworks. They can set their own examinations within the framework of guidelines of standards and requirements.'

Head teachers in Sweden have to meet so many explicit criteria before they 'choose' their own staff that it is said that candidates for teaching posts might just as well be picked by computer. Gunnar Thorsell, rector of Bromma Gymnasium in Stockholm, told the same conference of the society: 'On most of the matters where an English school is autonomous, a Swedish headmaster and staff are subject to constraints and limitations.'

'On most', but with the possible exception of the French system, English secondary school education is influenced more than any other by the requirements of external examinations. These in part replace the constraints laid down by local and central governments in other countries. Britain is the only place in the world which has a double-barrelled examination leading to university entry with (in England and Wales) its O Level and A Level examinations. The English and Welsh system is unique too in its early specialisation and narrow diet encouraged for children after the age of sixteen. This concentration on a specialist programme has meant that pupils start dropping subjects which may even include science, mathematics and modern languages as early as fourteen, a practice which would be unthinkable in other countries.

Scotland is closer to the broader Continental system. Pupils wishing to go on to higher education have to pass five subjects in the Higher Certificate and two of those will be taken at a more advanced stage. West German students have to contend with quotas being set by universities in certain disciplines. The competition to get onto these courses is very stiff and yet the *abitur* is a six-subject examination. In most *Länder*, German, mathematics, one modern language and a science are compulsory. Two of these subjects are increasingly being taken at a higher level by means of a different paper. The intricacies of the French *baccalauréat* defy description in a short chapter. All of the thirteen groups of subjects that can be taken include French, and most of them include mathematics and a modern language. In contrast it is possible to get into a university in England with two passes at A Level, so that after taking five or six or maybe as many as eleven or twelve subjects at O Level (or CSE) at sixteen, the English sixth former begins to specialise in three subjects.

The shining goal of O Level and A Level examination passes has meant that schools in England concentrate on academic rather than vocational subjects. Only about 20 per cent of 16—19-year-olds are still at school or college compared with 50—90 per cent in other European countries. Although the British Government through the Training Services Agency has made a start with vocational courses for these young people, it has some way to go to match the measures on the Continent. The government announced in June 1977 a £160m a year work-experience training programme for young people aged between sixteen and nineteen who are not able to get jobs within about six weeks of leaving school. This will go some way to redress the balance. However the extra vocational years on the Continent do not necessarily lead to better-qualified on the Continent do not necessarily lead to better-qualified school leavers. England and Wales, France and West Germany each have between 200,000 and 300,000 pupils leaving school every year without any qualifications.

In France the Association pour la Formation Profession-elle des Adults was set up in 1966 to undertake the major responsibility for vocational training and in 1968 it was running experimental courses for 200 young people. The next year the number on these courses had increased to 4,000. In 1971 an Act was passed giving employees the right to paid training. Since then a committee chaired by the

Prime Minister has been set up to review progress in vocational education. A permanent group of civil servants is concerned with vocational education and supplies the Prime Minister's committee with information. In 1975 the French spent £400 million on vocational training as compared with £251 million spent in Britain a year later. An appraisal of vocational education and training in France and West Germany carried out by the Training Services Agency in 1976 says: 'Throughout, the French vocational education system seems to be characterized by a lack of complacency.' Norman Newcombe, a British teacher who has sampled a variety of primary and secondary schools in five European countries besides England, wrote:

> Where the French programme differs from ours is in the provision of a very wide range of more or less vocational courses: Commercial Studies, various kinds of technical courses and so on. Perhaps we are too frightened in this country of letting our education have any vocational slant; our ideal seems to be the 'pure' rather than the 'applied' study. The French appear to have no such inhibitions (*Europe at School*, Methuen. 1977).

This amounts to saying that the English system, probably deliberately through O and A Level, has tried to protect the academic content of school education. This means that without a radical reform of the whole concept of O Level it is going to be extremely difficult to point able children in the direction of industry.

In France the technical slant has invaded the traditionally academic *baccalauréat*. Technical *baccalauréats* were introduced in 1969 and the proportion sitting them has risen from 12 per cent to 26 per cent of all *baccalauréat* candidates. A government campaign of building technical colleges has meant that in 1975, 569,000 students were attending these as compared with 2,600,000 in general education colleges.

In West Germany, although day-release to a training college is a right granted to all 16–18-year-olds, there is no question of parity of esteem between vocational and academic education. Members of the National Union of Students and others who during the Great Debate praised the Federal

Republic's day-release system may not have fully realised how rigidly divisive it still is. Nearly two-thirds of West German schoolchildren attend *Hauptschule* from the age of eleven upwards where teaching is barely above elementary school standards and strictly related to practical uses in later life. About 57 per cent of West German schoolchildren leave *Hauptschule* at the age of fifteen and enter the 'dual system' having obtained a three-year apprenticeship with some firm, so that they attend *Berufsschule* for one or two days while the rest of the week is spent in on-the-job training. Another 9 per cent (about 230,000 young people) who fail to get an apprenticeship have to attend *Berufsschule* part-time, although they are so little motivated that their attendance is poor. The Training Services Agency's report comments: 'It seems that because the German system is so well-defined with such precise legal distinctions, a labelling process which seems detrimental to many young people's self-respect is firmly established.'

Each year an increasing proportion of West Germany's young school leavers fail to obtain a satisfactory school-leaving certificate leading to future employment. Without this they can neither enter into an apprenticeship contract nor participate in any other state-run vocational training scheme. They are unable to enter any of the training occupations and must compete with guest workers from southern Europe, North Africa and Asia who are willing to work for low wages and short contracts, for any menial and unskilled work available.

As far as Italy is concerned, so many children are leaving school without any skills to face unemployment that pressure was brought on the Cabinet to approve a Bill in January 1977 making technology and practical manual work part of a compulsory core curriculum for 15—19-year-olds. In March 1975 the Swedish government introduced a Bill to make schools more responsive to the labour market. One of its features was to encourage work experience among pupils in upper secondary schools. Greece too is bringing in reforms to channel pupils towards technical and vocational courses and away from the academic tradition.

The shift away from the academic tradition, which is happening more slowly in Britain than in other European countries, is being accompanied in most of them alike by shouts of declining standards. West German employers have complained about school-leaver recruits who cannot do basic arithmetic. *Le Mond de l'éducation* complained recently about the large numbers of semi-literate and semi-numerate schoolchildren in the bottom streams of French secondary schools.

The Australian *Bulletin* in May 1976 exploded a great debate of its own when it leaked the findings of a two-volume study by the Australian Council for Educational Research of 13,000 Australian schoolchildren, half of them aged 10 and half of them aged 14. Eight per cent of the 10-year-olds did not know the alphabet, more than a quarter could not divided 56 by 7. But the 14-year-olds were not much better. Ten per cent could not tell the time on a watch showing 4.40; 5 per cent could not multiply seven by six; 22 per cent could not read a simple gauge such as is used on kitchen scales. Exactly half could not write 'correctly' a letter applying for a job. Correctness was judged on the student's 'shrewdness' in mentioning his address, actually saying he wanted the job, and remembering to sign his name at the bottom of the letter. The *Bulletin*, using the slogan 'We're turning out millions of dunces', pointed out that the Federal education budget had grown from $300 million in 1970—1 to $2,000 million in 1975—6. It said: 'It seems not unduly alarmist to say between a quarter and a half of Australian schoolchildren have very serious basic inabilities.' The report on Australia's 'education scandal' prompted enough correspondence to fill several volumes of further research. Most of it, the *Bulletin* said, was full of regret that the media had taken so long to recognise a disease which was widely seen as destroying young people's prospects and eroding the cultural and economic potential of the nation.

In Sweden a survey by the National Board of Education in 1975 showed that one 16-year-old out of five left Swedish schools with the basic skills of an average 13-year-old and about 5 per cent had little more ability than the average 11-year-old. A recent much smaller survey of numerical skills carried out in three Swedish schools showed that as many as one-fifth of the pupils there aged 15 and 16 could not add up two sets of three-digit numbers correctly. A new Centre—

Right coalition government was formed in September 1976 ending thirty-three years of Social Democratic rule. Mrs Britt Mogard, the new Education Minister, has announced that she intends to 'get back to basic subjects'.

In North America too there has been a great debate over standards. Enthusiasm for a curriculum or programme tailored to each individual child has steeply declined. The American Institutes of Research have carried out an immense study of 'progressive' methods of teaching and curriculum design, and have concluded that these innovations have not improved the achievements of pupils. Marks scored by school leavers in the Scholastic Aptitude Tests, taken by those wishing to proceed to higher education, were in fact shown to have fallen for the thirteenth year in succession.

In Ontario the Ministry of Education has already set out a new compulsory core curriculum and has announced that in future it will exercise greater control over what is taught in schools.

There is a legal aspect across the Atlantic too. A parent in 1976 sued the state of New Jersey on the grounds that his children could not read by the time they had left school, and that this was a breach of the state law which said that children were entitled to a 'thorough and efficient' education. Those administering education in the USA have to be constantly aware that school boards in North America can be liable for damages.

Concern about falling standards in North America has been partly caused by complaints from universities and colleges about their candidates, although the evidence from the Scholastic Aptitude Tests was ambiguous and confused. One could ask whether like was being compared with like; whether the notion of an *average* score made any sense, when probably more candidates and more socially deprived candidates were taking the tests each year. But, all the same, the evidence was widely accepted as indicating a need for schools to teach what the universities wanted, and what they wanted was a greater emphasis on English, mathematics and other basic subjects. Many states have already introduced mandatory tests for High School pupils to make sure they are actually learning what they are supposed to learn. This is a genuine innovation in the USA where, apart from the

Aptitude Tests, which in any case are not taken by everyone, pupils generally have been free from public examinations throughout their school careers. The introduction of testing can therefore be taken as a measure of the new anxiety. It is the state, not the teacher, which is now responsible for good education.

But how ready are different states to take on the new responsibility of restoring morale, raising standards and bringing about a clearly much needed shift from traditional academic bias (which suited a selected few) to an education of an equally high standard, but flexible enough to equip children of all abilities for a largely industrial society where jobs are increasingly competitive?

The Scandinavian highly bureaucratised education model is perhaps more suited to this responsibility than any other. It is small, spends a lot of money per child on education, and is highly controlled. Yet it has the disadvantage that curriculum development is so detached from teaching that it gives the teacher no scope for initiative or imagination. Consequently teachers become frustrated.

In the second model, West Germany, teachers are probably just as free, if not freer, than their British counterparts. But there is no mechanism for centralised change. In fact such change would be greatly feared and resisted by the *Länder* who have the spectre of a return to Nazi regimentation always before them. In any case curriculum development is so much the preserve of the universities and has such a high academic status that it seems doomed to lead out its life in ivory towers.

France, the third model, has most nearly achieved the education miracle of preserving academic standards yet embracing the demands of an industrial society. (Nearly half the age-group attempts the *baccalauréat*.) It has also established a system of effective communication between the centre and the periphery. It has taken and is taking steps to decentralise the system at the same time as the British Government, despite devolution, is making noises about centralising its education system.

Britain could learn a lot from France. The main difference between the two countries is that the mechanism for a central lead exists in France, whereas in England it exists but remains dormant. If it were mobilised as it should be, the English system as a whole would benefit from the strong tradition of teacher independence. The teachers would necessarily have the most important part to play in the new order and would be by tradition and temperament insistent on playing it, in contrast to the reluctance of their French colleagues to take on responsibilities.

3 Standards

'The debate about standards ought to be conducted according to the very highest standards of reasoned and penetrating consideration.'
— Sir Alex Smith, chairman of the Schools Council, in a letter to *The Times*, 9 July 1976.

The calling of the Great Debate in England and Wales was, as we saw in Chapter 1, a government reaction to widespread concern about falling standards of performance in schools. This concern, as we have also shown, is shared by other countries, notably North America, Australia and Sweden. Yet in no other country did the prime minister or president take a leading public role. So further discussion about the Great Debate must start where it all began — Ten Downing Street.

Before he became Prime Minister, Mr Callaghan was not noted for any profound utterances on the educational scene. When he succeeded Mr Wilson, members of *The Times Educational Supplement* staff frantically scanned all his past public speeches and remarks to see if there were any references to education. None were to be found. The answer supplied by Mr Callaghan's private office was that in his various roles as Chancellor of the Exchequer, Northern Ireland Secretary, Home Secretary and Foreign Secretary, he was never in a position to declare an interest in schools. This is true, but at times like general election campaigns, ministers are invited and able to stray from their departmental briefs. A correspondent of *The Times* who followed Mr Callaghan closely during the February 1974 campaign in his Cardiff constituency could not remember him voicing any concern about schools, at a time when the system was under greater pressure than at any time since the war.

So the Prime Minister's public interest in education expressed to Parliamentary colleagues soon after he moved to Number Ten appeared to have been new-found. He had not had a privileged education himself and is one of the two British prime ministers (Ramsay MacDonald, the Labour Party's first prime minister, being the other) to have gone completely through the working-class mill. His father, formerly a naval petty officer, died shortly after the First World War, and James Callaghan was sent to Portsmouth elementary and northern secondary schools. He was denied the chance of a university education, he told the House of Commons soon after becoming Prime Minister, because his family could not afford it. Mr Callaghan's two immediate predecessors – Mr Wilson and Mr Heath – had managed to get to university from modest backgrounds and may have thought that the bright child would win through in the end. Mr Callaghan, who had not been able to win through but had to leave school at sixteen to become a clerk in a tax office, was concerned that some bright children were being held back.

One of the roles he adopted shortly after becoming Prime Minister was that of the Common Man looking in at government policy from outside to see where there should be a shift of emphasis. He called in a number of ministers individually for wide-ranging chats about their departments and long-term policies. At that time not only were large numbers of employers, it seemed, complaining about illiterate and innumerate recruits and a shortage of school leavers skilled enough to be taken on apprenticeships, but it was also clear that at least half of the 150,000 young people leaving school that Whitsun were destined for a long stint of unemployment as they had few if any qualifications.

Mr Callaghan must have felt the irony of the situation strongly since Mr Mulley was the first minister to be called in for a tour of his department's policy, on 21 May 1976. During a two-hour talk, Mr Callaghan said he intended to make a series of speeches on education and he asked if the DES could brief him on four areas of particular

48

concern: the teaching of the three Rs in primary schools; the curriculum for older children in comprehensive schools; the examination system; and the general difficulties facing the 16—19-year-olds.

The Right were by now eloquently conducting the chorus of discontent. Mr Norman St John-Stevas, Conservative spokesman on education, who had promised a charter of rights for parents so that they could have a bigger say in schools, urged that HMIs should return to their proper role of inspecting, and called for an inquiry into comprehensive schools. Dr Rhodes Boyson had co-edited a fourth in the series of *Black Papers* calling for public tests in literacy and numeracy for all children at the ages of 7, 11, and 14.

Just as Mr Callaghan took over, a report by Dr Neville Bennett, of Lancaster University, was widely publicised and seemed to give factual support to theories about the fallacies of modern teaching methods. His tests showed that on average these methods delayed children at the upper end of the primary school from progressing in the basic skills by between three and five months.

Mr Callaghan's speech was widely interpreted in editorial articles in *The Times* and *The Times Educational Supplement* and elsewhere as stealing the clothes of the Conservatives, who had until then made all the headway in declaiming about poor standards of teaching. Mr Callaghan 'gathered his *Black Paper* cloak around him' as the *TES* rather Homerically described it, and led the Labour Party to share the national concern.

There was nothing new about fears of poor standards. As the Bullock Report on the teaching of reading and English pointed out in 1975, there never has been a time when people did not complain about poor standards in schools. In preparation for the Great Debate HMIs turned up an old quotation from Sir John Gorst, the last vice-president of the Privy Council's committee on education, who wrote in 1904 that there were 'millions of children in this country who, from their babyhood up to the age of 14, are drilled in reading, writing and arithmetic, upon a system, the result of which is that when they attain the age of 13 or 14 and are finally dismissed from school, they can neither read, nor write, nor cipher. . . .' Similarly a Ministry of Education report commented in 1952: 'The misgivings most often voiced during the year concerned standards and attainments in the three Rs especially Reading and Writing.'

Statistical grounds for believing that there had been a decline in the performance of children in the basic skills came in 1972 with the publication of a survey of 7,000 children aged between 11 and 15 by the National Foundation for Educational Research. The survey had been commissioned by the Government and carried out by Dr Brian Start and Mr Kim Wells, two members of the Foundation's staff. They gave reading tests to the children at 438 schools in 1970 and 1971 and compared the results with those obtained from using the same two tests in previous years. Their findings suggested that the steady progress of reading improvement maintained between 1948 and 1964 had been checked and that there were in 1971 more illiterate schoolchildren than there had been in 1964. (Start and Wells, *The Trend of Reading Standards*, NFER.)

The survey threw the concern over falling standards into the party-political arena. It was perhaps coincidental that 1964 should have been the date of Labour's victory in the general election. More perhaps than in other countries the Socialist Party in Britain became identified with free informal methods of teaching in primary schools leading to unstreamed and mixed-ability classes in comprehensive schools. The Socialists were therefore determined to prove that more children were passing public examinations and standards of achievement were rising. The Conservative Party became identified with traditional formal methods of teaching and with the retention of selection of academic children at 11-plus for grammar schools. They were therefore out to prove that the new approaches nurtured by the Socialists during six years of government had led to a decline in standards of performance.

The Great Debate gave the country its first opportunity to get away from this unfortunate and futile polarisation of educational beliefs and sterile attempt to relate ideologies to educational performance. To demonstrate just how sterile it was, we want to deal with it in three parts: primary school teaching methods, comprehensive schools and illiterate/innumerate school leavers.

Primary school teaching methods

The Start and Wells survey on reading standards was later
dismissed as 'blatant nonsense' in a critical review in the
NFER's magazine, *Educational Research*, published in June
1975. Miss Elizabeth Burke and Dr D. G. Lewis, of
Manchester University, said the tests used were twenty-three
and sixteen years old and showed signs of being dated. The
survey had not allowed for the influx of West Indian, Indian
and Pakistani children between 1964 and 1971 and had
concluded that there had been a decline in reading standards
merely because a predicted improvement had not taken
place.

A few months earlier the committee of inquiry under
Sir Alan, now Lord, Bullock, a former vice-chancellor of
Oxford University, had reported. It was set up by
Mrs Margaret Thatcher, then Secretary of State for Education
and Science, soon after the findings of the Start and Wells
survey had been published. The 600-page Bullock Report,
A Language for Life (HMSO, 1975), although long and, for a
report on language skills, not itself very engagingly written,
is still a better background document on education than any
produced for the Great Debate. It included a survey of 1,800
schools, and with one exception the committee of twenty
concluded: 'There is no firm evidence upon which to base
comparisons between standards of English today and those
of before the War, and the comparisons ventured are sometimes based on questionable assumptions. Nevertheless
standards of reading and writing need to be raised to fulfil
the increasingly exacting demands made upon them by
modern society.'

The committee were cautious, too, about the need for
imposing any particular teaching method. They found little
substance in the complaint that many schools were promoting creativity at the expense of basic skills. It was only bad
examples of 'discovery' or informal methods which had led
to trouble. Where the use of progressive methods was good,
results in literacy were also good.

This brings us to the report's one 'overriding conclusion'
which is so obvious that many might think it was needless
to state it. Yet it needed to be stated because it had become
lost in the conflicting warfare of battling ideologies. It was:

'There is nothing to equal in importance the quality and achievement of the individual teacher.'

Despite all the furore it caused, the report by Dr Bennett in April 1976 publishing the results of tests he gave in the three Rs to thirty-seven classes of children aged ten and eleven in Lancashire and Cumbria, illustrated the same point. The classes were divided between those taught formally and those taught informally. His report (*Teaching Styles and Pupil Progress*, Open Books) showed that on average those taught by the more traditional methods achieved significantly better results than those taught in small informal groups where children were much freer to talk and wander about the classroom. Its main message, which became lost in the predictable *Black Paper* chorus of approval for the work, was that planned and carefully structured teaching suited most types of pupils and that, provided there was a coherent programme, the teaching method was not all that important. The class in his survey which produced the best results was taught by a teacher using informal methods on a carefully structured basis.

The *Yellow Paper* (the DES secret memorandum to the Prime Minister, see Chapter 1) took up this point when it said that informal methods of teaching were satisfactory when used by skilled and experienced teachers. In his speech at Ruskin College the Prime Minister added that the methods were 'dubious' when they were not in such capable hands.

It is surprising that it took ten years or so after the Plowden Report for this point to be generally recognised. Bennett's research was the first serious attempt to introduce some evidence into the battle over primary school teaching methods. 'The only weapon not used,' he wrote, 'appears to be research evidence.' Like any serious investigator, he discovered that the distinctions between 'progressive' and 'traditional' were far too crude. Full-blown 'progressive methods' were not used exclusively in as many schools as had been thought. Most teachers used a mixture of both.

The futility of the debate over whether progressive methods mean declining standards was exposed. Dr Bennett made a plea for more sophisticated research into which teaching behaviours related to children's progress. It has yet to be taken up. The debate on standards continues: the

NFER carried out in 1976 the first part of a survey of the reading attainments of eleven-year-olds in England which suggested that standards had risen slightly between 1955 and 1976. No one should try to prove that this is a result of a swing to 'progressive methods'. No one should need to. Mr Callaghan's entry into the debate means that it should no longer be a party-political issue.

Comprehensive schools

Although the Labour governments of 1964 to 1970 zealously pushed ahead with the reorganisation of secondary schools along comprehensive lines, no socialist minister then or later has laid down criteria on which the comprehensive school programme could be judged a success other than that of successes in public examinations. This was the criterion of success used for the grammar schools, from which comprehensive schools were meant to be a departure. They were initially designed to be large enough for children to be given a wide range of course choices and the opportunity to follow their individual tailor-made programmes.

But examination passes are *not* the only measure of success and there are limitations to using them in the argument over standards and particularly in the controversy over whether the introduction of comprehensive schools has led to rising or falling standards. The fact that more young people are passing examinations now than a decade ago has probably more to do with the raising of the school leaving age in 1972–3 from 15 to 16 and with the introduction of the CSE examination than with any move towards comprehensive schooling.

Some examiners admit, too, to a tendency for examination boards to pass a fixed percentage, about two-thirds, of candidates in any subject. The complex difficulties of comparing grades given by examination boards over the years is amply demonstrated in a report by Dr Alan Willmott, principal research officer for the NFER, which was published in 1977 by the Schools Council. His findings that GCE boards were marking O Level candidates in 1973 on average a third of a grade higher than they did in 1968 are, he says, very tentative and in need of careful consideration.

A third limitation to using examination successes in this way was suggested by Professor George Thomas, professor of education at the University of Wales, Cardiff, and formerly an examiner for twenty-five years. He told the Welsh session of the Great Debate on 22 March:

> Too much has been made in the current debate of the number of passes attained by an increasing school population in various examinations during the last decade. I doubt whether the figures can prove a great deal either way. Over twenty years I doubt whether we are comparing like with like. To begin with, the increased numbers of candidates for public examinations seem to have produced a larger number of border-line cases for decisions by examiners. Further, the requirements to provide more examiners for the increased numbers has placed an excessive strain on the dwindling numbers of willing, experienced and suitably qualified examiners.

With these limitations in mind one should not become too much involved with a fruitless campaign to link examination failures to the growth of comprehensive schools. The first attempt to compare the examination results of comprehensive and grammar school systems was made by Mr Raymond Baldwin, director of a textile company and chairman of the governors of Manchester Grammar School, in October 1975. Mr Baldwin had already noted from his position on the city's education committee that students at the unreorganised Roman Catholic secondary modern and grammar schools were doing better in examinations than those at the city's ordinary maintained comprehensive state schools. Using his slide-rule on the national figures for examination passes published by the DES, Mr Baldwin now showed that pupils in the grammar/secondary modern school sector were getting more O and A Levels than pupils at comprehensive schools.

The Department made the mistake of rising to this bait and successive Labour Ministers trundled out examination results as if they were part of Holy Writ. In a debate on standards in the House of Commons in February 1977 just before the first regional conference Mrs Williams, for example, referred to a one per cent increase in the number of children with A Level passes and those with five or more O Level passes between 1964–5 and 1974–5. She pointed to a dramatic increase in the numbers passing CSE and said that now 80 per cent of all pupils left school with some qualifications, compared with 50 per cent in 1964—5.

But the quality of the latter part of this success story was dented by Baldwin returning to the fray in an article in the fifth of the *Black Paper* series (published in March 1977). He examined the examination passes between 1971 and 1974 and showed that the success rate at the level of five O Level passes and above had dropped in maintained schools although it had improved in independent schools during those four years. Statisticians at the Department hurriedly dug up the latest unpublished statistics for 1975 hoping for signs of a recovery but they only found confirmation of a further decline.

One man with his slide-rule (which Baldwin proudly said was his main calculating aid) had successfully countered the amateurish efforts of the Government to prove rising standards. His slide-rule could not, however, prove that a drop in examination results was purely or partly the result of the change-over to comprehensive schools. He tried by comparing the results in both grammar school and comprehensive sectors, even giving a handicap to the grammar schools to allow for 'creaming' by these schools of the brightest pupils from comprehensive schools in some areas. But the surviving grammar school strongholds are in the more prosperous die-hard Tory-controlled areas of England and Baldwin's findings could not take account of the fact that he was mainly comparing children from middle-class areas with those from working-class areas.

There may well have been a drop in the quality of examination passes between 1971 and 1975. Only time will tell whether it was because of the practical inconveniences of the rapid change-over to comprehensives that got under way during those years, or because of the initial effects of raising the school leaving age and forcing reluctant fifteen-year-olds to stay on at school or of the difficulties of local government reorganisation. Perhaps the most important factor was the high rate of teacher-turnover in those years, caused by low pay and a desire to get out of teaching posts in urban areas. A survey by the International Association for the Evaluation of Educational Achievement carried out among 258,000 pupils in twenty-one countries including Britain in 1970—1 should have shed some light. But the report, published in June 1976 by the Stockholm-based Association, said that home background had much more influence on educational achievement than type of school. It concluded: 'High selectivity (grammar schools) minimizes failure and low selectivity (comprehensive schools) maximizes success.' Even the Delphic Oracle could not have been more enigmatic.

A survey by HMIs on practice at ten good schools also found that success did not result so much from the way in which a school was organised as from effective leadership and the professional skills of head teachers and staff in creating a well-ordered school. The survey was produced as one of the background papers for the Great Debate. If it has been accepted by the two main political parties, then there is no further use in squabbling over comprehensive schools, and the Great Debate will have done this country a great service. For as Mr John Izbicki, Education Correspondent of *The Daily Telegraph*, a writer very much right of centre, told the Conservative Party in May 1977 during their version of the Great Debate, it was high time they accepted that 75 per cent, rising soon to 80 per cent, of the nation's children over the age of eleven were going to comprehensive schools.

Most of the political heat in government and local government in the last twenty years has been generated by arguments for and against comprehensive schools. It is a matter of little educational importance whether all children in an area attend the same school or go to different schools. The really important thing is that they should learn what they need to learn when they get there. Arguments to show that comprehensive schools *cannot* provide satisfactory educational environments or that they necessarily *will* do so seem equally futile. It is time to accept that most children in this country, as John Izbicki pointed out, will attend comprehensive schools and go on to discuss what they ought to learn there. More information is needed on the effects of different ways of teaching and organising classes. Perhaps some forms of structure and organisation, and some particular teaching methods and techniques make it easier for some children to learn than others. If so, we need to know what they are.

Illiterate/innumerate school leavers

There has been enough evidence of teenagers leaving schools illiterate and innumerate both here and in other countries to be alarming. Evidence is anecdotal, often based on impression rather than hard figures, but is still impressive and wide-ranging. It was provided both before and during the regional conferences and a few instances from the latter will suffice to indicate the breadth of this concern.

Mr Patrick Sharpe, a training director employed by a large firm, told the regional conference in Peterborough that only half of the applicants to his firm were able to get three or four simple sums right out of ten (example: 1,039 - 586). In Birmingham Mrs Renee Spector, who employs 100 unqualified school leavers, found that many of them could not read and could hardly write their names to get bus passes. Major-General Howell, director of Army education, told the regional conference at Exeter that the Army turned down three-quarters of its annual 43,000 applicants because they were not good enough educationally.

The suggestion that the calibre of recruits is not good enough today, whether for industry or elsewhere, is indisputable. The implication that this is because standards of educational provision have declined is highly controversial.

At the Cardiff regional conference Mr Peter Allen, managing director of the Welsh division of British Steel, referred to a report from the Welsh Confederation of British Industry which showed a dramatic increase in the number of applicants for craft apprenticeships who failed basic literacy and numeracy tests between 1966 and 1974.

The stock explanation was provided by Mr Fred Adams, director of education for South Glamorgan, that the potential craft apprentices of 1966 were now staying on at school to go into higher education. To this Mr Allen replied that it did not really matter *why* a poorer calibre of recruit was going into industry. What mattered was that this recruit was having to maintain and service plant in competition with the Japanese and other international competitors who had not had such a decline in the quality of their applicants.

This is the crux of the matter: the poor recruits are there irrespective of who is to blame — schools, parents, industry or the children themselves. Officials at the DES have shrugged off the evidence of employers as anecdotal. But the Department has commissioned no research on anecdotes which suggest an appalling situation in which hundreds, maybe thousands, of sixteen-year-olds are leaving school functionally illiterate or innumerate. As Shirley Williams said to the North of England Education Conference at Madeley College of Education in January 1977: 'There is no greater betrayal of a child than to fail to provide him with the basic skills he needs for work and for life.'

The proudest educational achievement by far of this Labour Government cost £1 million in 1975 and £1 million each year since and consisted of pump-priming a national campaign against adult illiteracy. It resulted (thanks also to the BBC's *On the Move* programmes) in the number of adults receiving help in one year jumping from 10,000 to 100,000. Now the Government should see what it can do for the adult innumerate. It may need a very different type of campaign. It should at least set aside enough money for research to find out why school leavers are missing out at school.

Then research might show how schools could help the future generations of adults so that they leave at least with the basic essentials. This must be the main priority of any education system. There are others and they must be defined in accordance with what the nation wants from its schools. Only after that can a debate be conducted, in Sir Alex Smith's words, 'according to the very highest standards of reasoned and penetrating consideration'.

4 The Curriculum

'Public interest is strong and legitimate and will be satisfied. We spend £6,000 million a year on education, so there will be discussion. But let it be rational.'
— Mr James Callaghan, the Prime Minister, Ruskin College, Oxford, 18 October 1976.

From a factual point of view the Great Debate hinges on priority being given to the basic skills in any new initiative in the curriculum. But from a philosophical point of view, can such a curriculum be justified? First, what is meant by 'curriculum'? We are using the word in its narrow and intelligible sense of what children should be taught at school.

Of course not everything that children or adults *learn* is actually *taught*. One may learn the taste of school rice pudding, or the meaning of boredom, or the most satisfactory part of the country to go for a walk in, without anyone teaching it. But it is confusing if such elements of learning are included in the concept of the curriculum, even if sometimes a distinction is drawn between the 'hidden' and 'overt' curriculum. One does, after all, continue to learn all one's life, at home, at work, as well as at school, college or university. But it would be absurd to speak of the things learned in these non-scholastic settings as forming a curriculum. Therefore we are confining our attention to the question: 'What should be taught? What should the timetable have in it?' Questions about the atmosphere or ethos of a school, the methods of teaching employed, the relationships between teachers and pupils or between pupils and pupils, although children learn from all these factors, are not

59

questions about the curriculum on our definition.

What, then, are the criteria by which one should decide on the inclusion or exclusion of any subject-matter in making up a curriculum? Every curriculum designer has tried to answer this question. Curriculum Studies and Curriculum Design have become major growth industries. Many thousands of words have been written and a wholly new vocabulary devised. It will doubtless seem foolhardy and ridiculous for us to try to give a short answer. But in theoretical and philosophical discussions short answers sometimes have their uses, especially if they are able to be understood. What we shall say will be obvious, even platitudinous. But platitudes can at least have the merit of being true.

Regarding education, then, as something which happens to most people mostly at school, and bearing in mind that people are not at school for the whole of their lives but must, by law, be there for part of their lives, the criteria for determining the school curriculum must be drawn from considering what is going to happen to the pupil after his schooldays. The curriculum designer must, as his first priority, consider the *future* of the people who are to follow the curriculum. Broadly speaking he must ask: 'Will the life of the schoolchild be better for learning the things which are to be included in the curriculum?'

Philosophers of education, notably R. S. Peters, have sometimes tried to derive certain basic ingredients of the curriculum from an analysis of the concept of education itself. This attempt has not been successful and is in any case confusing because it tends to conceal the nature of curriculum decisions. 'Education' looks like a concept which can be shown on purely empirical or factual grounds to apply or not to apply. If by the analysis of such a concept it could really be shown that a certain curriculum content was entailed, then one would only have to open people's eyes to the correct analysis of that concept for the curriculum content also to be accepted. So, for example, if you did not know what an opera was, you might dispute about what you were likely to hear when you were about to go to one. But once you had learnt about the concept of 'opera', then you would know that, whatever else you heard, you must be going to hear people singing.

60

In fact, of course, the concept 'education' is not like 'opera'. It slides about far more readily between the evaluative or loaded and the purely factual. Although it is possible to distinguish between bad education and good education, yet all the time there is a tendency to think that education is *really* good. So if it is argued that this, that, or the other must be included in the curriculum or the upshot will not constitute education at all (as one might say there must be elements of dramatised singing or the upshot will not be opera) one is concealing the evaluative nature of the argument. This is what is wrong with any such analytical approach to the curriculum. It looks factual, but is not.

The platitudinous criterion we offered above, on the other hand, namely whether the pupil's life will be better for having learned what is in the curriculum, carries its evaluative nature plainly on its face. And this is an advantage, for there is no doubt whatever that decisions about what is to be included and excluded from the curriculum are value decisions.

Are such decisions therefore political? Before the days of the Great Debate, the plea that politics should be kept out of education used to be heard often. Lately it has been heard a bit less. This is just as well, for the fact is that politics cannot be kept out. They are in there in the very nature of the case. But it is necessary to explain a bit further what this means.

Marxists argue that all value judgements of any kind are necessarily political, for they hold that politics is a matter of class struggle, so that any political activity is in fact a move in the class war. But they also hold that values, whether moral, aesthetic or more overtly social and political, are themselves the expressions of the ideology of class. In asserting that something or other is to be highly valued one is asserting an ideology and adopting a position in the class struggle. So for the Marxist it is absolutely self-evident that a discussion of what should or should not be taught at school is a political discussion. Any pretence that it is not is itself a mere move in the socio-political war.

We would dissent from this view — doubtless here rather crudely expressed. There are some value judgements, some beliefs about morals or aesthetics, which, though influenced

61

by the social and political provenance of their holder, can be debated and defended in a totally non-political way. To believe that something is good or better than something else is not always to hold a political belief.

On the other hand, in some circumstances such beliefs have to be implemented, not just privately among one or two people or within a family, but as a matter of public policy and with the use of legislation. At this stage a value judgement becomes a political one. For in such a case the question must arise as to who has the right to impose his views on other people by legislation.

Even if central or local government is proposing laws to protect the common good, which are agreed by all, political controversy could still arise if the laws required the spending of public money. People do not value only one thing, and priorities in public expenditure are bound to be political questions. Questions about education do concern priorities within one of the biggest government spending departments. As Mr Callaghan said at Ruskin College: 'We spend £6,000 million a year on education. So there will be discussion.' (The latest estimate from Mrs Shirley Williams in March 1977 increased the figure to £7,000 million, which is more than an eighth of all public spending.) In this sense certainly the Great Debate was intended to be a political debate and it arose in the context of politics. What people really mean when they say that politics should be kept out of education is that 'party politics' should be kept out of it.

It is certainly deplorable and inappropriate if the two main political parties develop such entrenched and dogmatic attitudes to educational policies that they each insist on promising to undo whatever has been done by the other, whether at national or local level. Party-political scrapping is peculiarly distasteful in circumstances in which individual children may suffer from the uncertainties and loss of confidence inevitably generated by constant threats of change.

The heated debates over comprehensive schooling are trivial, compared with the current debate about curriculum content. The excessive concentration in the past twenty years or so on the distribution and organisation of education has diverted attention from the central purpose of educational debate — namely to decide what it is that children need to be taught. The Great Debate, whatever else it may have been, was an expression of the wish to get back to this question.

Bad although party politics have been over the organisation of schools it will be far worse if they should now intrude into the classroom. The Great Debate has placed one of the highest responsibilities that could be placed on the leaders of the two major parties. They must agree on this matter. The warning that Mr Fred Jarvis, general secretary of the National Union of Teachers, gave when he read the reports of the *Yellow Paper* in October 1976 is a very apt one: 'Just think of the turmoil that would be created in schools, if we went from a Callaghan curriculum one year to the Thatcher theology in the next.' In this connexion it is comforting to hear members of opposed political parties agreeing with each other as Mrs Shirley Williams and Mr Norman St John-Stevas did when they appeared together on the televised version of the Great Debate on 3 February 1977. There is as yet no difference in the political stance of the two main parties on the curriculum.

But decisions on the curriculum will involve the expenditure of public money and will involve political decisions about priorities. For example, if there is a common agreement that schools should teach science to all pupils beyond the age of fourteen, then the question of providing sufficient laboratories in all schools arises. This priority might have to be weighed, in the present economic situation, against the fundamental one of providing 'roofs over heads' — places for children in schools — or money to employ enough teachers to keep the classes small.

We are asking the political parties to be united on the common aims of a curriculum. We cannot expect them to be united in their precise degree of commitment to those common aims, although we would hope they would agree on their importance. We hold the view that an attempt to stand at a distance and describe the 'goods' towards which education should be directed will make such agreement more, not less possible.

The test, we have said, of whether something should have a place in the curriculum is whether a child's life will be better after leaving school for having learned it. Very broadly, curriculum-makers have tended to concentrate on one of two possible functions of school. They have aimed to ensure either that school prepares a child for the tasks he has to perform when he leaves, or that the child has, for his own sake, 'grown' — fulfilled his potential, or developed a mind which is acquainted with different types of thought and experience.

The first view is, on the whole, old-fashioned. It is connected with elementary education for working-class children and education for leadership for public schoolboys, with neat sewing and domestic science for girls, and car-maintenance and metal-work for boys. It is exemplified by such writers as F. Bobbitt who, in his book *How to Make a Curriculum* proposed in 1924 to discover what to include in the curriculum by finding out what tasks there were in the world to be done. The second view is less utilitarian. It is derived from more up-to-date theories of knowledge and personality and is exemplified by such philosophers of education as Paul Hirst ('Liberal Education and the Nature of Knowledge' to be found in *The Philosophical Analysis of Education* edited by R. D. Archambault, Routledge and Kegan Paul 1965). It seems to us that neither of these approaches can be neglected. Both are relevant to the notion of the good life.

First, a life is better if it is a working life than if it is not. Perhaps a period of general and widespread unemployment opens one's eyes to the intrinsic merits of work. But whatever the cause it seems increasingly to be allowed that work is something valuable for itself, and not only for the monetary rewards it brings. Even if the work itself is boring it is more satisfactory to work for one's keep than to be given it for no work. The concept of earning or deserving one's pay-packet is important. The satisfaction of doing something, even exhausting oneself doing something which has to be done — a task waiting to be finished — cannot be treated lightly.

The vision of a world of increased leisure is one that is likely to be forced on us and one that some of us might regard as a nightmare. People with more leisure tend to find jobs to do, perhaps doing tasks which they might have employed other people to do, and so getting satisfaction both from the work and from 'earning' in that they have saved themselves some money.

Does anyone seriously dispute that it is better to work

than to be idle, and not morally better, but simply more enjoyable? It follows that a child at school must be prepared for work. He must learn what he needs to know in order to work, and Bobbitt's idea that one should find out by research what this is does not now seem so absurd as it did ten years ago.

What the pupil at school needs to know is largely determined by what other people need him to know. So one must resist the idea that teaching children at school what society needs them to know is somehow wicked. Children at school are also members of society. What children need and what society needs are two interlocking concepts. Often people speaking of this aspect of education use emotive expressions such as 'turning out fodder for industry'. Such expressions suggest that schools are in danger of becoming mindless factories using teachers as machines — or at best machine operators — to turn out pupils as inanimate products. They suggest further that industry itself is wholly destructive, like the cannon, of those fed into it. If one is seduced by these metaphors one forgets that it is in the interest of pupils themselves that they should be able to take an active working part in industrial society and that they should be fit to work in industry, though not only there.

The other somewhat less emotive word sometimes used of education which looks to the needs of society is 'vocational'. This too is misleading. To be prepared for work is not necessarily to be prepared for a particular *kind* of work. It is not necessary to learn the details of a particular job beforehand in order to be a well-prepared candidate for that job. Nor, in order to be well-prepared, is it necessary to know exactly what it is one is preparing for. In paying attention in general to the needs of possible employers one is not sacrificing the needs of the pupil; one is ensuring that they are met.

The needs of employers and possibly pupils alike may well entail a certain amount of knowledge about how workers can participate in the decision-making of industry. Whether or not all Lord Bullock's recommendations on industrial democracy are implemented, there is likely to be a move in this direction and schools have a long way to go to prepare for it. Mr Roy Jackson, education officer for the TUC, made

65

this point when he spoke at the regional conference at Newcastle upon Tyne. He said:

A hundred years of compulsory schooling has done little to inform young people about industrial society. They have not got the basic understanding and skills on which to begin to contribute to the running of our industrial enterprises. They are politically and economically illiterate in a society where most of the important decisions that affect the quality of their lives are made by others.

The second kind of determinant of the curriculum is equally important and in no way incompatible with the first. The other ingredient of the good life, besides work, is a capacity for pleasure (including, of course, pleasure in work). Some people are probably born with a greater capacity for pleasure or indeed for happiness than others. And some people's capacity may never be realised through ill fortune, poverty, bereavement or illness. But there are ways in which school can increase a child's capacity for pleasure, and these ways must not be neglected.

A child will increase his capacity for work, pleasure and leisure if he is, for example, a fluent reader or if he learns in some fairly precise and limited field what it is like to be an accurate observer and recorder of observations, or a good performer or viewer who can discriminate between what is well and what is shoddily done. A school will have done its work well if by means of the curriculum a pupil has learned to see more in things than meets the superficial eye; if he has learned enough of some things to find them of continuing interest; if his imagination has been so caught by something that he wants to go on with it by himself and become on his own account an expert.

A third, related, kind of external demand which determines the curriculum is the demand of higher education. No curriculum which failed to make provision for those who wanted to proceed to higher education could possibly be satisfactory. The numbers of those wanting to go on into higher education are continuing to increase. Dr Aubrey Trotman-Dickinson, Vice-Chancellor of the University of Wales, Cardiff, told the Welsh regional conference: 'The universities and polytechnics are together probably the greatest single consumers of the school product in that some 15 per cent of children in the age group now go to them. It is important that these people are now given the maximum opportunity to develop themselves to be intellectually stretched throughout school life.'

It is right that there should be this degree of dependence of schools on places of higher education. It would be a disaster for education in general if schools broke away and attempted to become independent of colleges and universities, setting their own standards and dictating their own curricula without reference to what higher education wants. Schools are of course part of the general educational provision, and may well, as they do, discuss curricular matters with universities and polytechnics. But if any education is to be taken seriously then higher education must be.

In meeting all these needs the school is preparing the pupil for one thing: independence. It may sound rather odd to equate independence with work. But, in our view, the worker is freer than the person who does not work and who has to be dependent on unemployment benefit or on an institution. If one has learned to take pleasure in a wide range of activities, one's freedom is also increased. If one is given the opportunity of getting a higher education, one is given the opportunity of greater intellectual freedom. The crucial point in curriculum-building must be to ensure that none of these aspects of freedom is forgotten.

Before we go on to consider the particular and practical implications of these demands on the curriculum, there is a very important point to be dealt with. Who are we to say that curriculum-makers must bear these needs in mind? If educational curricula incorporate values, as we have argued, then why do we suppose that our values are those which are to be preferred? Why our ideology rather than any other? Are not all values and ideologies on the same footing? What seems good to us may not seem so to anyone else; and what seems good to Rhodes Boyson may not appeal to Michael Young. There is no such thing as an absolutely right set of values, so to search after a consensus is absurd; but to try to invent an ideology which is to be adopted without any consensus is arrogant if not totalitarian in spirit.

A consensus about what is the good or the common good is probably impossible. In a time of acute national crisis such as war it is almost possible to believe in the reality of consensus or the general will, because the common good is reduced to some fairly clear though negative aims: to avoid defeat, to resist invasion, to ensure that supplies do not run out. But when the storm is past, the idea of a Rousseauesque General Will evaporates. And then someone has to decide what should be done.

But to say that there is no general will, no absolutely agreed common good, is not to say that any view is as good as any other. Values are not wholly relative, and in practice no one believes that they are. Nice things, as Kingsley Amis said, are nicer than nasty things. It is impossible, if you sincerely believe that something is good, or important, at the same time to think 'and it may not be', and 'those who think differently may well be right'. Such modest protestations that one's own view has nothing special to recommend it are appropriate only in the very different case of guesswork, or of opinion formed in the clear knowledge that evidence is lacking. 'Your guess is as good as mine' is a way of suggesting that there is no known answer to the question in hand. But when one actually claims *knowledge* one cannot also hold that someone else's contrary claim is just as good.

As with knowledge, so with the statement of values. There are some things which are genuinely matters of taste or of opinion and are known to be such. These are the judgements we make and can quite happily preface with the words: 'I prefer . . .', or 'As far as I am concerned . . .', or other phrases to disclaim dogmatism. But although we know that people's moral views differ and that they value things differently, yet in seriously stating a value judgement or making a moral claim, we cannot at the same time suggest that anyone else's views, though the opposite of our own, might be as good. Asserting a value is asserting it as *to be preferred*.

If then, as we have said, decisions on the curriculum contain implicit value judgements there is no question of making such a decision and at the same time holding sincerely that any other decision might be just as good. Obviously one might agree that details could be differently worked out or that other means to the same end might be adopted. But to specify criteria for forming a curriculum is to claim that some things *ought* to be taught. And to claim this is to claim superiority for one's own ideology. Nor is it surprising to discover that the ideology we have suggested is, broadly speaking, bourgeois. When we speak of the needs of children and the needs of society interlocking, we are thinking of society as it is, a mixed-economy society, part socialist, part capitalist, with a strong bias towards individual liberty. We think of individuals motivated by a desire to work, a desire to earn, a desire to better themselves. We think of the criteria for good education as determined by the bourgeois work-ethic and the ethic of independent thought and free imagination. Such criteria will inevitably be rejected by those who are ideologically opposed to existing society, the location of power within it, and the existing balance between free individuals and authority. There is, and must be, a conflict between those teachers who want to abandon bourgeois goals and establish altogether new ones, and those who feel a commitment to and responsibility towards existing institutions and society as it is (though such teachers may not necessarily be uncritical of society, nor opposed to piecemeal reform).

Our contention is that, until the government of the country is itself committed to a total revolution in society (and then only if the government has been democratically elected), institutions such as schools and, for instance, broadcasting, are bound to reflect the values of existing society.

There is therefore something naïve about those young teachers who claim they are being open-minded at the same time as they claim the need for an alternative curriculum to replace the 'old hierarchical, dictatorial, subject-orientated curriculum'. (See for example Nigel Wright on 'Teacher Politics and Educational Change', in *Explorations in the Politics of School Knowledge*, ed. Geoffrey Whitty and Michael Young.)

Someone has to make the decisions, to recognise that they are value decisions, and to stand by them. There is bound to be paternalism in education, and paternalism is rightly exercised by the elected source of power. The government

has to impose on people *for their good*. The bold words of
J. S. Mill (*On Liberty*: Introduction) that neither government nor public opinion has *any* right to impose a way of
life on another for his own good cannot be wholly endorsed
by any responsible government. If a government has been
democratically elected, it must take this right to itself,
namely to interpret the general good. But the means of
imposing its interpretation on people may not always be by
legislation. (In the case of education, decisions can be better
implemented by the issuing of curriculum guidelines, by the
examination of pupils, and by co-operation and discussion
between government and local education authorities, or
other relevant bodies, such as examination boards, and
finally by the control of finance.)

There is a parallel here between education and health. If a
government believes that it is necessary for the sake of public
health to have regulations about the preparation of food, for
example, or the tipping of rubbish, then these regulations
are made and public health inspectors are appointed to see
that they are carried out. Health, though in some ways an
imprecise concept, is one which is universally acknowledged
to be a good, both for its own sake and for the sake of its
consequences for the individual and for the community.
Government is therefore charged with the responsibility of
safeguarding it as much as possible by, for example,
advertising the risks of such practices as smoking and so on.
The goods which result from education, the freedoms which
we have tried to set out above, seem to us to be of the same
kind. If so, then it is the responsibility of government to
see that they are protected in plans for the education of
children.

But, of course, wherever a government has to be paternalistic there is inevitably tension between authority and freedom.
In the realm of medicine, for instance, it is easy to see how
the more imaginative a government becomes about
preventative medicine, the more individual people may feel
that their freedom is being undermined. Similarly the
spectacle of central government intervening in the curriculum
caused at the beginning of the Great Debate a chorus of
protest against possible totalitarianism, regimentation and
other evils. But although understandable, the outcry was

misplaced, for *someone* has to make the curriculum decisions.
The government has the role of promoting the education of
the people, and it must in a democratic country take such
decisions both in the interests of the people and as the voice
of the people at large.

After all, as we have already pointed out, central government has to allocate money to education. It has to weigh up
education as a whole among its priorities, such as health,
highways and defence. It is absurd to suppose that a government can do such weighing up properly while taking no view
whatever on the nature of the education on offer. Once again
we have perhaps become blind to this obvious point over the
last twenty years because of the undue concentration on the
administrative and organisational aspects of education. While
governments were taken up with the questions of selecting
pupils at eleven and of comprehensive schools, it seemed
possible to assume that what was actually taught at school
was somehow a package the contents of which they could
take for granted. We have tried in Chapter 1 to trace the
history of the shift of responsibility for educational provision
to a point where as far as central government was concerned
it had allowed education to become like health: a general
good to be distributed.

Our criteria, general as they are, would probably not
command complete agreement even if they were broadcast
to the nation and printed in the front of every school textbook, or on every notice board, or written large on the
walls of the Schools Council in Great Portland Street, or
on the Poulson-designed edifice of the DES's offices at
Waterloo. But they serve as an example of the *kind* of general
statement of value which it is expected that a government
should make.

Having stated the questions which ought to be asked and
answered about the curriculum, the government should set
about seeing whether actual curricula do or do not satisfy
these criteria. Obviously there will be tension in this activity.
It would be both depressing and surprising if there were not.
For, as we have seen, there are many other parties in any
dispute about what is to be taught; and above all the teachers,
who rightly think of themselves as experts, will dislike being
dictated to. The more professional they are, the less they will

like it. But it is the existence of this kind of tension which is the dynamic in education.

Moreover, deciding on the criteria by which a curriculum should be judged is not yet to decide on a curriculum. Just as Bentham thought that in the Greatest Happiness of the Greatest Number principle he had provided a test against which systems of legislation and individual laws could be measured, so the Government should have a principle, a known and understood and consistent set of criteria, to apply to the curriculum on offer in schools. But this is not to say that they and they alone should lay down the details of the curriculum.

Being paternalistic, then, means being brave enough to provide guidelines for the curriculum and devising ways of seeing that these guidelines are followed in schools, otherwise they will at best be pious hopes. These guidelines must be drawn up in accordance with our general criteria. Her Majesty's Inspectors could ask of a school and with regard to individual pupils in a school the kinds of question we have suggested. Is the child actually benefiting in the ways that he should? Is he learning what his future employers or educators demand that he should? The essential feature of these questions is that they should look to the future. They recognise that being educated is not an end in itself, but for most people a temporary phase whose justification lies in the nature of life as a whole. They are questions which can be asked equally about the education of the most and the least able child. For the hope of work and the enlightenment of the imaginative understanding of the world are goals for everyone, even though the kind of work and the degree of understanding may be enormously different for different children. In this sense the curriculum for all children should be the same; it should lead in the same direction, even though some may get further along the road than others.

But though it seems obvious that one must have a theoretical basis for any intervention, or indeed for any criticism of existing curricula at school, merely to have this is not enough. The curriculum debate would not have lasted long, nor seemed more than an exchange of pieties, if more had not been intended. It is now time to see whether the criteria we have suggested for determining curriculum-content have any positive consequences. Would anything follow from the general adoption of such criteria? How specific should the guidelines be? We shall attempt to answer these questions in the next chapter.

5 The Inner Core

'I must state at the outset my categorical belief that *a great number of teachers* in this country would welcome more positive guidance on a core curriculum. They recognize a need to satisfy the community that everything possible is being done to provide every child with the fullest possible opportunity to be literate, numerate and to have an understanding of society.'
— Mr Ron Cocking, treasurer of the NAS/UWT, Birmingham, 18 March 1977.

A theoretical consideration of the criteria by which to devise a curriculum leads directly, as did the practical consideration, to the need for a curriculum to be devised around basic skills which schools are compelled to follow. But what do we mean by compulsion? There is no need, for example, for Section I of the 1944 Education Act to be changed. It is the duty of the Secretary of State to promote the education of the people. The Secretary of State already can and does, if he or she wishes, provide more 'positive guidance' on the curriculum. Whether that guidance is followed by schools should *not* be a matter for legislation. Some of it will be a matter for examinations and the rest for the inspectorate and local authority advisers. Therefore when we discuss in this chapter and the next which elements in the curriculum should be compulsory, we are not thinking of legal compulsion. All the actual content of the curriculum should be outside the legislative arena. So the clauses in the Act making religious education statutory should be repealed.

The case of religious education will serve to illustrate our

general contention. It should be retained, as will be argued
later, as a compulsory element in the curriculum. But we
agree on balance with those church bodies and religious
education teachers who have asked for the 1944 regulations
to be lifted. Legislation is not the right vehicle for ensuring
that the value decisions which the Secretary of State makes
about the curriculum are adhered to.

In the first place, as can be seen with religious education,
legislation can be and is ignored. Any law which can be
flouted by five schools out of six needs to be reconsidered.
Legal imposition of the curriculum is quite rightly resisted
by the teacher unions. And Mrs Shirley Williams has made
it quite clear that she has no intention of resorting to this.

Secondly, although morals are not totally relative to a
certain time and place, they do nevertheless reflect public
opinion. Value decisions which reflect public opinion
should be capable of being changed, even if gradually. A
curriculum based on such value decisions must be flexible.
A curriculum stereotyped in a volume of educational law
(or *Läroplan* as in Sweden) is not flexible. — *Striked*

When in 1944 the government laid down a statutory
duty on schools to hold daily religious assemblies and to
include a weekly element of Religious Education (RE) in the
syllabus, England could still have been regarded as a nation
of churchgoers and believers. There were far more active
members of Christian churches than there are today. Arguments for religious education now depend more on the
concept of the needs of the pupil than on any special place
which religion has in the official life of the country. Therefore religion should be no more legislated for than literature
or physical education or any other part of the curriculum.

Spiritual needs are not promoted by legislation. Sometimes,
it could be argued, they are held back if the result of legislation is the unedifying spectacle of non-committed
Christians, atheists, and even some of those opposed to
Christianity, holding Christian or other assemblies which
bear little relation to actual religious events. It does not help
the cause much, either, when there are desperate efforts to
use the RE statutory slot in the timetable for something that
will be a bit of a rest from maths or games. — *Seen as an easy*
Religious education is the only requirement for the curric- *way out*

ulum laid down by legislation in this country. Legislation has not done the *promotion* of religion much good. Lord Longford, speaking during a House of Lords debate in February 1977, said the law was being flagrantly broken on a wide scale and one of the reasons for this was a shortage of teachers. Laws cannot force teachers to become religious education specialists even at a time of high teacher unemployment. So legislation is not a weapon the Government should use to promote that 'paternalistic' responsibility for education which we described in the last chapter as 'being brave enough to provide guidelines for the curriculum'. The Government should be prepared to make clear what it thinks is right and to use such measures, short of legislation, as it thinks will be effective to enforce it.

If the Government's guidelines for the curriculum are to be based on the criteria we suggested in the last chapter then there must be a common curriculum which would apply in all schools. It could be argued that since one of the criteria we mention is concerned with children's needs, and since all children are different, there should be a different curriculum for each child, based on his particular needs — a set of 'individual programmes', to use the American phrase. A commitment to mixed-ability teaching can be used to reinforce this argument. For since it is impossible to teach children of very different capacities the same things at the same time, some theorists make a virtue out of necessity (or out of dogma) and argue that each child should have his own curriculum objective and pursue it in his own way under the guidance of his teachers.

It is an ideal which in Britain's present economic climate is not likely to be reached. Lord Alexander, former secretary of the Association of Education Committees (AEC), dismissed mixed-ability teaching on those grounds. 'You need a very skilled teacher,' he told us. 'It needs individual tuition. We cannot afford this.'

But there are philosophical as well as practical considerations against tailor-made curricula. Children are certainly different in the uninteresting sense that Mary Smith is not identically the same as John Jones. This means that there may be a place for individual programmes in the classroom. But in more important respects children are the same. Their needs as members of society are the same. They share capacities to work and to enjoy the fruits of their imagination. The demands made by employers and institutes of further and higher education apply equally.

These of course make up the list of criteria laid down in the previous chapter as those on which government guidelines should be based. The needs of the children must in the first place be subsumed into the needs of society if both are to be met. The needs of society are common. The curriculum should be common if it is to meet them. The Government should lay down a common curriculum, not the teachers, although they should be directly involved. It is not that some alien force — Industry, Big Business, the Barons, the Churches, or the Establishment — should dictate what teachers should do. Children are members of this society just as much as their parents, their future employers and, for that matter, teachers themselves. Government must be the interpreter of the wishes of this society.

Dr Harry Judge, director of the department of educational studies, Oxford University, has argued that the concept of a central core curriculum for schools is an irrelevance and should be abandoned as soon as possible (*New Society,* 21 October 1976). Instead, he suggests, the performance of schools should be monitored and assessed. The notion of the common core gave rise, he wrote, to too many intractable political problems.

We profoundly disagree: precisely because the question of what should be taught as the common curriculum is political it is therefore relevant and cannot be avoided. The common core is what society demands that children should learn. Teachers as responsible members of society must teach this.

But who are we to step in where Dr Judge fears to tread and to define what we think should make up that common core? It is obvious that we are not experts in curriculum theory and we are not pretending to be. In the last fifteen years there has been a growth in the number of university departments of education. This growth has produced a great deal of research, and has given birth to whole new subjects which have gained in respectability. Whereas the theory of education used to be a separate and despised area with only vague connexions on the one hand with social history and on the other hand with some fairly 'soft' philosophy, now by its marriage to sociology it has taken an entirely new aspect. The field of Curriculum Theory has its own language, its own methodology, and its own aspirations to scientific status.

We are not concerned with such theory. Education is practical and inextricably political. The values of society have to be embodied in what is taught at school, in curriculum practice, otherwise the mis-match between school and real life, which has given rise to this present sense of crisis, cannot but increase, for Curriculum Theory is in danger of becoming a world of its own. Just as legal theory is often very different from legal practice, so while sociologists and educationists may seek to analyse curricula, and set up forms of 'value-free evaluation' (an odd-sounding phrase) or 'illuminative' evaluation which makes no judgements (just two examples from M. D. Shipman — 'Contrasting views of a curriculum project,' *Curriculum Studies* 1972), we do not feel inhibited by being outside this world.

Common sense demands a common curriculum which will satisfy the needs of those who follow it, is capable of being evaluated, and can be tested to see if it is working for the good of those following it, as members of society. If it is not; if it is out of date, or biased towards the arts, or insufficiently geared towards the acquisition of useful skills; if it is unintelligible or causes great boredom, then it must be judged deficient. Such judgements cannot be wholly scientific. They must be made by reference to what children know, what they can do, whether they enjoy themselves, and whether too many of them are frustrated and limited when they leave school. Curriculum judgements, like other political judgements, must be based on a combination of sensitivity, ordinary knowledge and an understanding of people's actual wants and needs. If theory can contribute to such understanding, it can be used. If not, it must be abandoned.

Abandoning theory may not be too painful, because on the whole there has been a general common-sense agreement about the basic essentials of the curriculum which has picked out those foundations upon which all other learning and competence must rest. This core — 'irreducible minimum', as the Government's background paper to the Great Debate called it — is already part of the curriculum in every school.

78

So if it became compulsory and subject to a compulsory examination it might make a difference of emphasis in schools, but it should not introduce anything radically new.

The aim of a core curriculum is simple: to ensure that children as far as possible are equipped to exercise freedom of choice both within their education and after they have left school. In order to pursue their individual goals at school and afterwards, they need to have followed a basic curriculum. They *need* to have been taught the basic skills whether they *want* to learn them or not.

What then should be included? Literacy and numeracy automatically and by universal agreement have a place on the list of essential subjects. But even here things are not as simple as they look.

To start with literacy: those people who suggest that it is dead, that the age of reading is past, must be joking. It is true that there are now other ways of learning about things than by reading about them. But then there always were: you could hear about them. It is true that television has made it possible to learn *more* without reading; it is also true that, partly because of television, fewer people than before read for pleasure. But these facts do not make it less essential for children to be able to read, if they are to exercise their freedom. And they must be able to read more than just street-signs and instructions on fire-extinguishers. They must be taught to read with a certain initial understanding. The other aspect of literacy is to be capable of writing.

An 'educated person' can write, and write in such a way as to be understood. It would be very strange if the desirability of writing had to be defended in detail. To many people it would seem almost a contradiction that one should be able to think but not to write — difficult and laborious as writing may often be. Writing intelligibly requires effort: it needs the mastery of syntax of the language; it needs an extension of vocabulary beyond the normally or casually spoken range; it needs a grasp of punctuation and a moderate acquaintance with spelling. All these have to be taught and taught with patience. One of the main lessons from the Bennett Report (see Chapter 1) was that this kind of formal teaching did not lessen a child's ability to write creatively. Nor was this ability promoted by informal teaching.

It has been held that an insistence on correct syntax and correct spelling is a middle-class obsession. Working-class children will not, it is claimed, ever need to write much, and if they do they should write their own language. The same has been argued with regard to immigrants. But such arguments will not really stand up to examination in a society one of whose professed aims is to diminish class differences and to integrate immigrants into society. Nothing could be more patronising than to suggest that in deprived areas people should have to rely on others to do their writing for them. Are there to be no working-class journalists, novelists, lawyers or broadcasters? (For it should not be forgotten how much broadcasting is parasitic upon writing or for that matter upon reading.)

In fact this is an area in which, above all, the needs of society and the needs of children at school are identical. For society needs writers, journalists, television and radio programme-makers, as well as people who can take minutes at meetings, draw up plans, correct school books, argue about education and even write White Papers. There is no end to the need for writers as well as readers. Therefore the language must be reasonably well understood; its demands must be accepted and its difficulties tackled by those who are going to use it. Abuses of syntactical coherence and of punctuation make it more difficult to understand language, and diminish its usefulness.

Literacy means not only being able to read but to write and to write properly. We shall return to the question of reading later. For reading is not only useful: it is a source of infinite pleasure. As a source of pleasure it should be taught and encouraged, but not examined. Its practical use can and should, however, be subject to examination with the rest of the core.

Numeracy should also, by general agreement, be part of the central core, but here too there are problems. Some, such as Mr Eric Midwinter, of the National Consumers' Association, think that its importance has been exaggerated. He is inclined to believe that the rhetoric of the three Rs and the purely verbal satisfaction of the twins — numeracy and literacy — have made people assume without question that numbers are as important as letters. However, he would not

80

want to exclude at least some basic mathematics from its central position. From an individual point of view literacy may be more important, but the demands of modern society have elevated numeracy alongside literacy as an essential of equal importance.

In everyday life there is a need to calculate fast, both at home and at work. In work people are more likely to use calculators regularly. More important perhaps are the humdrum and domestic demands on people's powers of calculation. Without the ability to multiply and divide with reasonable speed and accuracy the task of buying curtain material, or of working out how much carpet one will need for a room or seed for a lawn would be formidable indeed. Even if the person at home or at work has a calculator, there is still a need to calculate how to use a calculator. This entails a basic and sound knowledge of mathematics.

The need for speed and accuracy is an argument for learning multiplication tables. There is no substitute for this. Samuel Pepys was struck by the magnificence of tables when he was first introduced to them, and rightly saw that they had endless uses. But to argue that children at primary school should learn tables and perhaps glimpse some of the magnificence that Pepys saw in them does not mean that they should learn them to the exclusion of everything else. Nor does it mean they have to learn them in unison chanting two-two's-are-four etc., though this has its place and may be much enjoyed. Many schools already teach a judicious blend of traditional and modern mathematics, and such a blend is increasingly becoming recognised in O Level examination syllabuses. This blend would seem to be the most useful, as well as the most fruitful, mathematical curriculum.

One of the faults of 'new maths' in its early days was that none of the textbooks, including the original School Mathematics Project (SMP) books, contained anything like enough examples and exercises. Teachers, who were themselves beginners in the subject, were hard put to it to devise exercises for themselves. Consequently children often went on from one topic to the next with no real grasp of what they were supposed to have learned, or what could be done with it.

In the learning of mathematics, repetition and a wealth of examples are not boring. They are the only ways a child can feel confident that he has truly grasped a process. To feel sure that you can do something, that you at least know how to set about solving a problem, is just as satisfactory as feeling that you have some grasp of the logic of Venn diagrams, or some understanding of number-theory. The pleasures of getting things right must not be underestimated. The dichotomy between learning by rote and repetition on the one hand and insight and understanding on the other has been a false and damaging one. The fanatics who spread this false dichotomy are now fewer in the field than they were. The inspectors used to be some of the worst offenders. Under the formidable leadership of Miss Ethel Biggs, they did much to introduce new maths into the schools, and then, still under her guidance, began to advise caution and the mixing of topics and methods. Most of the worst failures in mathematics teaching are now the result of the inadequacies rather than the dogmatism of teachers. Whatever method is used, and whatever topics are covered, only a teacher with some mathematical insight can begin to teach even quite young children to understand what they are doing in their maths classes.

The third element in the compulsory core curriculum should be elementary science. As in the case of mathematics there is a balance to be struck here between what is theoretically likely to serve as a foundation for further study and what is practically useful. More weight should be placed on the practical aspects at this stage. It is absurd that children should live all the time among artefacts which they actually have to use every day without having any idea of how they work or indeed what they are.

We envisage a science syllabus (or more properly a range of syllabuses) which starts from the objects — the electric plug, the switch, the telephone, the internal combustion engine, the radio receiver, the television set, etc., — and in each case works from the particular to the more general. In this way a practical competence should with luck and good teaching lead to the beginnings of theoretical understanding.

The children who at present have most chance to learn any practical subjects are the least able. All children should have this chance. This does not mean cooking and woodwork but practical, elementary technology. Professor Bernard Crick, in his inaugural lecture (a much belated one) as Professor of Politics at Birkbeck College, London, in January 1977 spoke of a common-core curriculum divided between 'knowledge' and 'practicality'. He said: 'By practicality I simply mean that an educated man should be able to tackle most of the small technical problems that he meets in everyday life. The schools should aim to nurture a technological spirit and competence in practical ways.'

The fourth and last element in the compulsory core curriculum should be a foreign language. We take the view, shared to a large extent by the inspectorate, that modern language teaching in English schools is a disgrace. If we are serious members of the Common Market, now is the time when this must be changed. There is a great deal of expertise in the teaching of languages in non-academic institutions, including language schools of various kinds. This expertise should be deployed. Children should be taught to talk in at least one other language besides their own for their own sakes and for the sake of society.

Professor George Steiner, of the University of Geneva, has repeatedly said that the English nation by being a nation of linguistic illiterates is damaging its own chances of economic survival. Children must be taught to speak a foreign language confidently, fluently and in such a way that they are eager to learn more both of that language and others. French is taught at most schools as if it were a dead rather than a living language. Far too much emphasis is paid to writing rather than conversation. Even pupils who proceed to A Level or French degree courses are often totally inhibited from speaking the language, despite their knowledge of French literature.

One should not be dogmatic about the age at which a second language should be started, nor about which language should be chosen. French is firmly entrenched in most schools. But large schools should offer German and Spanish as well, from the beginning, so that a child can choose which second language to acquire. An experiment to teach French in primary schools failed in the 1960s, but as Dr Clare Burstall, deputy director of the NFER, pointed out in her report (*Primary French in the Balance*, NFER, December 1974), this was partly because the children had to learn the same things all over again in the secondary schools. Enliven the teaching and there would be a strong case for reviving primary school French, and, if it is possible, starting primary school German and Spanish. But enlivening the teaching does not mean watering down the linguistic content.

A new style of teaching and therefore of testing must be developed as a matter of urgency. The emphasis should be put squarely on understanding the spoken word and conducting conversations even of a simple kind. This should be compulsory.

The teaching of languages as part of the core curriculum leads us to a final point of fundamental importance. The core is for everyone, whatever their ability, in an ordinary classroom in an ordinary school. In such schools the range of ability is extremely wide, and with the move towards the integration of handicapped children into ordinary schools, the range will become even wider. The handicapped children who are to be integrated will not all be bright spastics or partially-hearing children of normal intelligence. They will be the mildly educationally subnormal (according to the present system of classification), the maladjusted (most of whom also have learning difficulties) and many others. The core curriculum is the right curriculum for all children including the handicapped, for these children, as much as any, need to be given the basic skills they can use as members of society.

But it is of the essence of handicap that the child who suffers it usually needs to be taught far more than other children. He needs perhaps to be taught things which other children pick up without teaching, such as how to talk. So although a core curriculum examination may well serve as a goal for the very unable, it may be one they can never reach. It may well be, for example, that the time spent on reading, writing and calculating (leaving time for the other parts of the curriculum which have still to be discussed) will leave no time for learning another language, which would in any case be confusing and beyond the intellectual grasp of the less able child.

This child should be examined in what he has done and

should be able to leave out some parts of the curriculum altogether. This would involve the school in some decision-taking: those children who are not up to a second language should be excused it. But those who are, should have to learn it properly. The growth of the fools' option — European Studies or whatever else it is called — in which everyone looks at pretty pictures of French markets and shops must be avoided. Otherwise no one learns to speak the language at all.

Mr John Townshend, senior lecturer at Hertfordshire college of higher education, wrote in the *TES* (15 April 1977) that the development of European Studies courses was a 'measure of the failure to come to terms with the teaching of French to the less able'. In the same edition of the *TES*, Mr Michael Taylor, from St Benedict's comprehensive school, Colchester, wrote:

> The pen of my Aunt is banished from the classroom because it offends the new secularism; it is odd. Learners may no longer ponder its oddity and the light it throws on the nature of language. Yet as our maligned forebears knew, to encourage such . . . reflection was to teach French, and something more than French as well.

6 The Middle Circle

'I don't think you can understand our society unless you
know something about the Christian religion. This country
has been nominally Christian for so long it has had considerable effect on the law, customs and people's attitudes. I
don't think you can understand the world in which we live
unless you have some concept of the part religion has played
in it.'
— Sir Ronald Gould, former general secretary of the
National Union of Teachers, interviewed 2 February 1977.

It is fashionable to draw diagrams to illustrate curriculum
structure. We could draw a very simple one: three concentric
circles. The innermost, smallest circle surrounds the compulsory core curriculum of subjects or skills which can be
tested. It was discussed and defended in the last chapter (reading, writing, mathematics, science and a foreign language).
The third circle would contain optional subjects. The middle
circle would encompass subjects which should be compulsory
but cannot be subjected to public examination.

It is with regard to these last subjects that the role of guidelines laid down by central government is most important.
Where there is an examination to be taken, the subject-
matter to be examined is certain to be taught, and if the
examination is publicly and centrally or regionally examined,
then the standard of teaching, though bound to vary, will on
the whole be high. All teachers will want to do their best for
their pupils, and to see that they pass the obligatory tests.
But where there is no examination, the only way to ensure
that the subjects are taught is through inspection (whether

locally or centrally initiated), by exhortation and support. Much depends here on the role of the local advisory service and its relation to Her Majesty's Inspectorate which will be discussed further in Chapter 9.

Local authorities vary very greatly among themselves as to how strong an advisory service they maintain and in what subject areas. They also differ in respect of how much money they would be able to spend on backing up schools which wanted to bring the curriculum into line with the recommendations, on providing new resources and in-service training for teachers already in post. There is something to be said for earmarked grants from central government to local authorities, deeply though these would be resented and fiercely as they would be resisted. Such grants would not be a threat to local power, so much as a guarantee that money earmarked for education through national negotiations between the government and local authorities (in the Rate Support Grant process) would actually be spent on education. We cannot see any other way in which guidelines laid down by central government, and allocated for in financial terms, can be followed as they should.

But to return to our concentric circles of the curriculum: the second circle of compulsory subjects to be taught in all schools is a matter of far more controversy than the first. We want to put forward in this chapter some candidates, all of which ought to be begun in primary school and continued until the end of the third year of secondary school. We shall then discuss the third circle of optional subjects from which pupils should be able to choose more freely as they move up the school. There is no particular order of priority in which to discuss the non-examinable compulsory subjects. Not one has been included which is not genuinely essential if the criteria outlined in Chapter 4 are to be satisfied.

To start with the non-controversial: there is probably no need to go through elaborate arguments to justify the inclusion of physical education (PE) in the compulsory but non-examined circle. Perhaps because of the tradition of boarding schools in which a child's whole life was taken in hand by his teachers, British schools have never thought that only intellectual activities should be included in the curriculum. However, considering the criterion of future benefit to the child, some part of PE teaching should be concerned to introduce him or her to activities which could be easily kept up after school, such as swimming, tennis, golf, or badminton. Many schools are already very enterprising in this matter and provide facilities which can be enjoyed by grown-ups from the surrounding community, so that schoolchildren and adults from the community can mix more freely.

At the opposite end of the scale of controversy comes religious education. It should not, as was argued in the previous chapter, be included in the curriculum by law; it should be part of our middle circle. By religious education we mean education in Christianity, and there are powerful arguments for keeping this in the compulsory part of the curriculum. If it were removed, it would continue to be taught in some schools. It would obviously retain its place in the denominational schools and in the many independent schools which are church foundations or have strong religious traditions. In those schools and perhaps in a few others it might remain as an optional examination subject. But it would not be a part of the common culture of the country; nor would religious knowledge of any kind be part of the common knowledge of all children. Of course it is not now. One has only to talk to anyone who teaches English literature to hear how complicated it is trying to read, say, *Paradise Lost* with pupils who have never heard of the Fall, or Original Sin, or to discuss *Ash Wednesday* with a class where some pupils do not know what Lent or Easter mean.

This ignorance is widespread in spite of religious education being a legally compulsory subject. But this is because schools have in fact given up all responsibility for teaching about Christianity, even if they have conformed to the law by having a slot in the timetable marked 'RE'. Many schools now insert a bit of casuistical discussion about moral issues, or some information about alternative religions and moralities, or else offer some opportunity for frank discussions of personal problems and put it into this slot.

The time is ripe for a complete change of attitude towards the teaching of religion. In the days when most people would have claimed to be a member of some church or other, it was obviously important, especially to parents, that their children should not be indoctrinated with beliefs drawn from a sect other than their own. Teachers had to be careful not to speak with the voice of the Methodist or the Church of England. If they had discussions in class, they were usually discussions about atheism or agnosticism. Children had Doubts (having doubts was a recognised hazard of adolescence) some of which were indulged, others less respected. But the whole of the teaching was undertaken in a general atmosphere of assumed religion.

To teach in such a way now would be absurd. One must today assume a complete ignorance of religion and a total scepticism about the necessity for there being any. The field is open to start all over again and introduce children to the idea of religion *from scratch*. This must be done through the medium of Christianity, even if a large number of children in a class do not come from Christian countries. The reason for this is that Christianity still exists as an institution in this country; its history is totally interwoven with the history not only of this country but of Europe as a whole. It is equally crucial to the study of all the arts, and of such institutions as the monarchy, Parliament and of course the Church itself. As Sir Ronald Gould said, any child who is being educated in England could not possibly understand his own environment without understanding something about Christianity (although he made it clear it should not be a compulsory subject). To teach about Christianity in this sense, however, entails teaching about Christian doctrine and the gospels and at least part of the Old Testament as the source and background of that doctrine.

Because of the new attitude to religion in society, a renaissance of religious education is timely. One no longer has to try desperately to make religion something which, though familiar, needs to be tarted up a bit to make it more exciting and relevant. Religious education need not be treated as an effort to give new interest to something which has become tedious through repetition. (Too often in the past the spirit of both RE and Assembly was that of wartime recipe books: *How to make something new of Carrots* and *Cabbage, too, can be a Delicacy* or other such titles.)

The time is ripe to treat religion as something strange, something quite outside the ordinary run of life, something which mysteriously has had a vast effect on people, over which wars were fought and people were burnt and persecuted, and which still has an effect on people, taking them on pilgrimages and retreats, something which cannot be reduced to just do-gooding at the Old People's parties or helping the neighbours; something, in fact, which has inspired some of the most beautiful painting, writing, music and architecture ever to be produced by the human imagination. Because the whole language and conceptual content of Christianity is so largely unfamiliar, it can be presented all over again as a source of inspiration, both as presenting a moral idea and as an attitude to human life as a whole.

The modern trend in theology — the recognition of Christianity as a myth, and the recognition of a myth as a way of presenting truth — makes possible the non-dogmatic but exact and concentrated teaching of Christianity in schools. If some of the children find that the gospels contain truth, then that is well and good. But, for those who do not, there is still the *phenomenon* of Christianity to reflect upon — to love or to hate; but at least they can acquire some knowledge of it.

The only people who would be incapable of teaching religious education in this way would be those who are actively hostile to the concept of any religion at all, who are totally committed to a mechanistic account of the universe as a whole, or who are themselves too ignorant of the Bible or too insensitive to its language to be able to interest themselves in the matter. Teachers of religious education need not be just the churchgoers and the believers, although these would be most suitable to teach the subject. They could be teachers whose main subjects at university or college had been music or history of art, history, or philosophy. Discussions on history, art, music and morality would all be equally likely to arise in the context of these lessons. The areas of religious education would be opened up to far more teachers, and this would go some way to relieving a national shortage.

The justification for teaching religion as a compulsory subject, then, is two-fold: first, so that children may have the knowledge necessary for them to understand an essential background to literature, language and institutions in the

90

country in which they live, and second, so that their own imaginations may be exercised on a dimension of life which is the proper concern of all religions. There is no other subject in the compulsory part of the curriculum which is designed to give them this kind of insight or to open up to them glimpses of this dimension. We believe that those who make the value judgements in accordance with which education is determined should be bold enough to assert the value of this dimension.

Far less controversial than religious education is the suggestion that some broadly aesthetic subjects should be included in the compulsory curriculum. A child's imaginative life is impoverished if he is not introduced at an early stage to aesthetic experience. But there are three important goals and none of them should be lost to sight. First, the child should learn to enjoy the experience of looking, listening, reading, and in general attending to other people's works of art, past and present. Secondly, he should at least begin to learn the skills necessary for creating his own aesthetic objects, and thirdly, with the help of these skills he should be able to express himself if he wants to. Any curriculum in aesthetic subjects which omits any one of these three is defective. There is nothing but frustration and boredom ahead for those children who are forced to express themselves but do not want to (and why should they?) and for others who are keen to do so, but have not the materials, equipment or instruments to do so intelligibly. It is an evasion of responsibility and a gross denial of potential pleasure to themselves and to others if this aspect of education is neglected.

Music is in a very special position here, since learning a skill may lead directly to learning about the work of composers. It is absurd to expect children to *become* composers unless they have at least some knowledge of the requirements of musical composition, and they can have the pleasures and discipline of expressing themselves by actually playing and singing the works of others. So it is a mistake to hustle them into composition, even improvisation, without a good deal of actual teaching of technique as a preliminary. After all, although some schools may not be able to afford many instruments (and it is extraordinarily

91

difficult to decide how much money should be spent on instruments which will be used only by a part of the school), every child in the school has a voice. Some can sing naturally, others can sing if they are taught. Even the toughest classes have been known to come to order and sing 'Edelweiss' and other songs from *The Sound of Music* like tame canaries. Rodgers and Hammerstein may not be Verdi, but one of the saddest things is to see children at school bored or rowdy in music classes because no one has ever taught them to sing, or introduced them to the pleasures of music. It is ironic when they listen with such enjoyment to music much of their waking hours outside the classroom that teachers do not do more to capitalise on this love by gradually turning it into a wider knowledge of musical form, and breaking down the ignorant snobbishness that divides 'good' from 'popular' music. Such television programmes as *All You Need is Love* (London Weekend, Spring 1977) show the way admirably.

Some might wonder why it is necessary to spend time justifying the inclusion of such subjects as music and art in the curriculum. Surely they are included anyway and all we are doing is telling our 'grandmother' teachers how to suck eggs? But are they included? A report by the National Children's Bureau, published in September 1976, of 16,000 children aged sixteen, included the results of a questionnaire asking what subjects they had studied at school. Nearly half (47 per cent) said they had never studied music and a quarter said they had never studied art. The replies, the report says, may not be able to be taken at face value. But even if more had in fact studied art or music, the replies did not suggest that the subject had made much impact on many hundreds of thousands of British schoolchildren, nor did it speak well of the breadth of some school curricula.

Art and music should be compulsory elements of the curriculum for all children at primary school and for at least the first three years at secondary school. After that they should be optional. Those who are keen will go on anyway and should be old enough to have a more professional approach. The case of literature is different. Reading, in the sense of being able to read to understand in a straightforward way, as well as to write intelligibly, has been included in the compulsory core which is subject to examination. But there is a whole range of experience which every school should provide for its pupils, and which should not be examined, and this is the experience of reading for pleasure.

Fewer children read for pleasure now than in 1939. A nationwide survey of 8,000 children carried out by the Schools Council in 1974 found that children were reading half as many books as they did before the Second World War and that two boys out of five aged fourteen and over did not read any books at all in their spare time. Individual children lose an enormous amount of potential imaginative life if they do not read for pleasure. Once children can read they ought to be given a chance to go on and read what they want to read. What stops children enjoying reading is its association with something done only at school, and then all too often with having to analyse what they have read and to answer questions about it. The spectacle of a child of twelve or thirteen who has thoroughly enjoyed reading a book quite fast, but who is then driven to despair by having to answer the terrible question: 'What can I say about it?' is far too common.

Far more time should be allotted in school to reading what a child chooses to read with no obligation at all to say *anything* about it afterwards. If, in the beginning, all the children wanted to read was comics and annuals, this would not be a disaster. At least some children would be starting to read and might be persuaded to read books that they might not otherwise have read. A good teacher can suggest and share his own pleasure in books without exercising censorship or compulsion. To be totally absorbed by reading a story, even rather a bad one, is better than never reading at all. Indeed, it is one of the major pleasures of life, and it is part of a school's duty to take it into account and to prepare children for it. Here then is an essential part of the curriculum, according to the initial criteria, and one which, of its very nature, must remain unexamined and untested.

Another completely different field in which there should be quite precise guidelines for a common curriculum is that of sex education. We believe that most parents wish such education to be undertaken at school, but that on the whole they would be far happier to know that there was some fairly precisely agreed syllabus so that their children would not be exposed to particular whims or fancies on the part of the teacher to whom the task of sex education happened to have been assigned. Here, above all, there would be much to be said for a central body of advisers, teachers, and national inspectors, to commission a series of television programmes which parents could preview if they wanted to.

The length of time that a course in sex education should take, the way in which it should fit in with other parts of the curriculum, would be matters for the school to decide. (Is it part of social sciences, or biological sciences, or religious and moral education, or perhaps all three?) All these things would be decided according to the general ethos of the school. What should be laid down, as it has been for the past few years by the French Government, is that some sex education should be given. We would suggest that it should start in primary schools. In such a controversial area there are manifest advantages in having a common syllabus agreed by teachers on a regional basis about which parents would have a chance to make known their views.

Perhaps the most important element of our middle circle, and the one about which there would be most agreement, has been left to the end. It is what Mr Patrick Martin, headmaster of Warwick School, referred to in the Birmingham regional conference as 'learning for life'. Mr Donald Frith, headmaster of Archbishop Holgate's School, York, told the conference at Bradford that there was a 'new area' in the curriculum. He said: 'It is learning about present day society, how the nation earns its living, political, economic and even personal ways of life. It used to be called "civics".'

The same kind of suggestion was heard over and over again. Mr Gerald Sanctuary, of the Law Society, told the London conference: 'Most young people are going to get married and get a job. They are going to go into some kind of living accommodation. They should know their rights and responsibilities. They are going to start buying things which go wrong; they may get into trouble on the roads; they should know what their rights are.'

Mr Eric Midwinter told us that the third element in the curriculum after literacy and numeracy should be teaching children what their role in society is, their role as consumers,

94

as the recipients of mass media communication, as parents, as workers. He insisted that the point of such education was not so much to prepare children to be members of society but to demonstrate to them that they were already members of society, and to enable them to appreciate what that entails.

'Social studies' is probably the most harmless name for this crucial part of the curriculum. Alongside religious education it should start when a child is five and continue at least until he is sixteen, perhaps even into the sixth form. In the later years, after the end of the third year of secondary school, it should include time for individual careers advice. Learning about the demands of work in general can be taught in the classroom. Learning about the demands of a job on a particular person must be communicated separately. Careers advice must be compulsory by the middle of a child's secondary school career. Even if a child is destined for higher education, he should know what jobs require which qualifications. Those who are going to leave without many qualifications should be told realistically what their opportunities are. If their opportunities are minimal, they should be told so frankly.

Much of the content of the social studies syllabus must be left to the school and should depend partly on the locality of the school and partly on the interests, prejudices and enthusiasms of the teachers. It would be part of such a course, if possible, to teach about the industrial, agricultural and archaeological history of the neighbourhood. It should include lessons on the social and political institutions which affect the child's life. Part should be devoted to criticism of the taken-for-granted features of the child's life such as advertisements, pop music, and television programmes. Surveys show that people are spending a great deal of their leisure time sitting in front of the television. Professor Richard Whitfield, professor of education at Aston University, has estimated that each of us will spend on average no less than seven years watching the box before we gather our retirement pensions. Over the eleven years of compulsory school from the age of five, the equivalent of one whole year of a child's life is spent watching television. (Aston Educational Enquiry Monograph No. 6.)

95

Every aspect of the environment, natural and artificial, in which the teacher was interested should have its part. In some respects the studies might be historical. (Exactly what is the Cabinet? How long has the TUC been in existence and what were the first trade unions like? What were the original assumptions and presumed duties of the BBC? Were there always laws governing advertising? How did Association Football grow up?) The School Council's joint industrial project with the TUC and CBI would certainly be part of what we are advocating.

There is no end to the misconceptions of which children are capable. Grown-ups find it hard to believe that children often think of everything that happened even immediately before they (the children) were born as equally ancient and remote as the Industrial Revolution or the Bronze Age. Social studies are absolutely crucial for people who are going not only to vote at eighteen, but to take part in worker participation. These kinds of studies, far more even than a nodding acquaintance with technology, will interest children in entering the world of commerce and industry, or if they reject it when they leave school or college, to reject it not through ignorance but through a fairly sound knowledge that it would not be the world for them. They will have been brought up to think of such questions as what the economy depends on, the alternative means of financing newspapers, television and radio, or how one can combine popularity in the media or in the production of consumer goods with good value and quality. Far too many children now, not only from private schools but from maintained schools as well, despise commerce and industry because throughout the whole of their school lives they have been led to think of 'cultural' topics such as Beethoven, Shakespeare and Rembrandt but never to think critically about their own culture, in the sense of what they breathe and live with every day.

Some people may never come across Shakespeare, but if they go, for example, to Langdon Park School, East London, they will come across Poplar because they will live there. They should learn about the running down of the area around the school — the closing down of East India Docks, of the hospital, of a special school and the threat to jobs. They should learn about the red-letter events in the area's history — the battle of Dodd Street in 1885, when 70,000 people demonstrated over the right to hold a meeting, the match girls' strike of 1888, the dock strikes between 1880 and 1920, the part the neighbourhood played in the General Strike of 1926, the battle of Cuba Street in 1936 when workers stopped one of Sir Oswald Mosley's marches, and so on. The area in which such famous figures as George Lansbury, the MP and Socialist Minister, lived is steeped in history which can be made to come alive. Of course it will be full of socialist content and some people might regard it as political indoctrination. This will depend on how it is taught, at what ages the socialist content is emphasised, how candid the teacher is in revealing his own feelings. He should generate his own enthusiasm among children and he should encourage them to question his views. For it should be a part of such a course that gradually, as he gets older, a child should learn to distinguish strong feeling from blind prejudice, reasoned argument from dogmatic assertion, and to respect other people's views. The neutral teacher has no part here — the teacher must be, above all, honest.

We are not advocating the early views of Midwinter that working-class children must be educated in working-class culture, but rather that all children of all classes and all ability ranges should be set to exercise their critical and discriminating intelligence upon the common as well as the uncommon features of their lives. The neighbourhood can be used to lead on to a wider perspective of the world outside.

Here a great deal of help can be given by television and radio-based teaching. Central government through its inspectorate or the Schools Council, or local authorities through the local advisers, could commission programmes to be made by the BBC or commercial companies. They could compile a list of topics which in broad terms they would like to see covered. These programmes would then be made as usual by professionals with complete freedom to treat the topics as they wanted to, subject to the general control exercised by the BBC's charter and the Independent Television Act. In this way it would be certain that the subjects were actually there in the curriculum for the schools to study.

A plan of this kind would mean that schools should all

possess video-cassette machines, adequate storage for tapes and at least one competent technician. These essentials should be universal by now, and if they are not, local authorities ought to put the situation right, however short their finances. Schools should be exempted from normal copyright laws so that they could tape and store ordinary 'non-educational' programmes for ten or so years. Both historical sense and powers of criticism (particularly media criticism) could be enormously strengthened by intelligent use of ordinary television and radio programmes, as well as schools broadcasts.

As with religious education, any teacher who was of a lively and inquisitive disposition could teach social studies of this kind. Many would be delighted to do so. Such studies must be seen by the head of the school and by all the staff as genuinely compulsory. Teachers should be made to feel that their reputation depended on their attention to these studies just as much as on examination results.

Finally, we come to the third circle, the optional subjects. These should be chosen from as wide a range as the size and resources of the school allow. We shall discuss the examining of these subjects at O and A Level in the next chapter. Some element of science and mathematics and of language-usage subjects should be continued as long as the child remains at school, for at least a small part of the timetable. Apart from these subjects a child should choose what he studies with advice from his teachers and parents about the ways in which his choice will relate to his needs later on. For some children the compulsory subjects, with perhaps one or two optional subjects, would in fact occupy all their time until they left school. For others choice and specialisation would start when they were fourteen or possibly before, if their general level of competence in the inner core subjects allowed it. These brighter children could choose another language, more sciences, English literature (which as a serious critical study would be a specialist subject), history, geography, more mathematics or a combination of these.

But while there should be a certain amount of choice in all schools, a school should not be judged entirely according to the range of choices available to a child. When comprehensive education was first being advocated, one of the advantages

alleged to flow from it was the wide range of choices open to
sixth-form students at large schools. This was soon proved to
be illusory. Resources in large schools had to be shared
between the academic sixth-form and the remedial groups. It
was quite common to find a small grammar school of about
500 pupils offering a choice of twenty-five or more subjects
at A Level, while a comprehensive school of 2,000 might
offer only ten or twelve. The lack of choice of subject is not
actually fatal even to the brightest child. He may be unable
to read Russian or study botany or ancient history or Greek
at school; but if he is academically inclined, he will enjoy and
profit from French or chemistry or modern history just as
much. After all, academic children are faced sometimes
with the agonising prospect of giving up subjects they have
enjoyed at some stage of their lives. They will have moments
of longing to have done everything, or at least the things they
never studied. But they are not really deprived. Choice, even
if it is possible, is often made for absurd reasons including
love of the Latin teacher or a vague wish to do (or not to do)
what one's father did. Sometimes other considerations, such
as the more personal atmosphere of a smaller school, are
far more important than the apparently restrictive choice of
O and A Level subjects.

There is a great advantage in allowing different systems of
education for those over the age of sixteen to exist side by
side and for certain schools to specialise in certain subjects
at the sixth-form level. Then, if a child wanted to do three
science subjects of which one or two were not offered at
his school, it should be normal routine for him to leave his
school and go either to another in the same area or to a
college of further education to pursue the subjects of his
choice.

There is not much to be said in favour of sixth-form
colleges. If a child is going to leave his secondary school, he
would do better to go either to another school, where he
could fit in with a group which was already known to the
teaching staff and well-established (new blood in a school at
the sixth-form stage is agreeable for everyone concerned),
or he should go to the more adult environment of a college
of further education where he will be doing his O or A Levels
alongside not only contempories from other schools, but

grown-ups studying to sit technical and professional examinations. Sixth-form colleges only serve to denude the schools of the most ambitious teachers (or some of them). They have a curiously impermanent feeling, because the pupils all come and go so quickly, and they lack the cohesive family nature of a good all-through secondary school for 11–18-year-olds. Given our lack of enthusiasm for vast ranges of choice, we do not share the present Government's sympathy for the general concept of the sixth-form college.

7 Examinations

'However, present arrangements and the modifications of
them now being considered will not answer two of the
criticisms commonly voiced today. The first of these is linked
to concern over competence in basic skills in mathematics
and the use of English, and leads to the suggestion that tests
should be taken by all pupils before they leave schools to
establish their competence in these respects. The second . . .
focuses on the fact that it is at present possible for
candidates to pursue some subjects to examination level
and to abandon others, considered by the critics to be of
greater (or more central) importance.'
— *Educating Our Children*, background paper supplied by
the Department of Education and Science for the regional
conferences.

The connexion between curriculum control and testing on a
national basis is of crucial importance. If curriculum content
is not to be enforced by law, as was argued in Chapter 5,
then what is taught must be externally tested, or else the guidelines, which it is the duty of the Government to lay down,
will be nothing but pious hopes. It is not enough for central
or local government to monitor the system as a whole through
such machinery as the Assessment of Performance Unit.
Monitoring is in effect very often not much more than seeing
how a system works, rather than seeing that it is working
properly. To be sure that children are actually learning at
their different schools what they should be learning, it is
essential that *they* — the individual children — should be
tested by an external system of examinations, in a way

that is broadly comparable across the country.

It has often been argued that examinations exercise a 'tyranny' over the curriculum; they not only frighten and inhibit pupils, but are also socially divisive. This kind of view was put forward, for example, in the Schools Council Working Paper 52 (published 1975) *The Whole Curriculum 13—16*). This paper quoted with approval the words of the Beloe Report (1960) out of which CSE arose: 'The examination dictates the curriculum and cannot do otherwise; it confines experiment, limits free choice of subject, encourages wrong values in the classroom.'

'Don't turn our schools into testing factories', Mr Max Morris, of the National Union of Teachers, told the regional conference in London. 'Any mad rush to a battery of tests and monitoring techniques would not be in the interests of the children', Miss Margaret Maden, headmistress of Islington Green comprehensive school, London, warned in Peterborough. Mr Jack Bainbridge, a senior inspector for Sunderland education authority, during the slide-show he gave to the Newcastle regional conference, wittily showed one of a school staff room in which the teachers were saying: 'We don't have much time for teaching here, we are too busy examining!' These warnings were reiterated by many teachers and educational administrators, not least of all by officials at the Schools Council when we met them.

The notion of assessment arises out of the child-centred and learning-for-yourself methods of the 1950s and 1960s. Working Paper No. 53 says: 'A concept of assessment is required which enlarges the framework of criteria against which educational performance is defined and evaluated and which brings a greater part of it under critical scrutiny.'

But whose 'educational performance'? That of the teacher or that of the pupil? Assessment — according to Working Paper No. 53 — ought to be such as to offer teachers 'reasonably accurate indication of how their pupils' basic skills compare with those of pupils in other classes or schools'. With the aid of such tests teachers can correct weaknesses in a whole group before they become too pronounced. They can, says the paper, place new pupils in appropriate groups; and they can group children in a way which is likely to ensure that they work well together.

102

Pupils themselves will learn from the tests to judge their own potentialities realistically, and parents will get guidance on how their children should proceed from one stage of education to the next. Such assessment, so the paper argues, will be mainly descriptive, and will have little in common with the old type of examination in which some do worse than others, even fail. The aim will be to discriminate not between different levels of achievement but between different levels of *competence* [our italics].

Even the Schools Council's working party which produced Paper 53 offered it as a discussion document rather than as a set of proposals which they expected their parent council immediately to adopt. Paper 53 virtually admitted that teachers, parents and employers all preferred the old-style examination which seemed to give those who were successful a positive certificate of success. Had the working party's proposals been adopted an immediate result would have been a much greater trend for employers, as many do now, to use their own tests for selecting pupils at 16-plus. Certainly employers could not be expected to put much faith in an examination system which tried to provide parity of esteem between different 'levels of competence'. What they are looking for is proof of achievement, which they can identify, however crudely, in formal examination grades and passes.

It is wrong to say that no one must sit old-fashioned examinations because some will not be able to attempt them and others are likely to fail them. The working party's paper was particularly anxious that the examination system should not perpetuate a 'divisive curriculum'. Here, then, in the end is a purely social reason for deciding an educational matter. Educational reasons should be put first in the educational context and, as we shall explain later, in the context of the curriculum for the 13—16-year-olds, there are sound *educational* reasons for splitting children into groups.

The Working Paper points out that about a quarter of the nation's children leave school without any qualifications to show for eleven years of compulsory schooling, and suggests that schools should build up profiles on all children which can be used when they pass from one stage of schooling to the next and from school to work. This is a good idea. There would have to be, though, some form of standardisation in the way the profiles are constructed so that they could be compared with others across the country. But profiles should not replace examinations.

The traditional merits of external examinations have often been rehearsed. The main thing is that examinations offer an incentive, a stimulus to teachers and pupils to work in a well-ordered way to defeat the examiners as a common enemy. Some would contend that this applies only to well-motivated, bright, academically-orientated pupils. Our impression from talking to teachers is that it can apply to other children just as much.

Dr Trevor Jones, chief adviser for South Glamorgan, an area which has the unfortunate distinction of the highest rate of truancy in England and Wales, told us in relation to CSE Mode 3: 'We do know from heads of schools that if there is an examination, people will turn up for it.' Mrs Margaret Fisk, head of compensatory education at Ivy Bank comprehensive school, Burnley, Lancashire, who teaches small groups of socially disadvantaged and disruptive children, said: 'There are no tests at present which are suitable to examine the type of child that I am getting. But a return to the School Certificate would give them something to aim for. A lot of children opt out because they have no incentive.' This sort of view has been confirmed by conversations with former pupils of special schools for the maladjusted. Over and over again they have said that they wanted a chance to take external examinations, even though they admitted that they might not pass them.

The second case for examinations is that there must be some form of local and regional standardised measurement in addition to the tests that teachers devise for their own pupils to check what is being learned and who is falling behind. The case for this was best put by Mr Conrad Rainbow, chief educational officer for Lancashire, an authority which is already in the process of using standardised tests for children at the ages of nine and thirteen in mathematics and English. At the Birmingham regional conference he said: 'The authority will for the first time have positive evidence on which to base its many decisions, on which to distribute its resources. Too many educational decisions are based on hunch and inspired guesswork.'

The third case rests on the need for national measurement, and national measurement now, which entails national comparability. We have already discussed the limitations of examination successes as pointers to national standards of schoolchildren's performance. Whatever their disadvantages something is needed to counter the present crisis of confidence in the nation's schools. We cannot wait another few years for the Assessment of Performance Unit to come up with more sophisticated, but probably less popularly intelligible, measurements. It is easy for politically-motivated groups to produce inconclusive evidence to show that standards are 'crumbling'. There must be ammunition to keep up the morale of the teachers and counter distorted facts and the frequent complaint that teachers are not accountable. At least one central part of the meaning of 'accountability' is that those who are accountable should be able to render an intelligible account to the interested public.

We are *not*, however, suggesting that individual schools should publish the results of their examinations. In an ideal world we would encourage this and accept the advice given by Bernard Levin to the head teachers of Andover, Hampshire, to publish and be damned (*The Times*, 10 August 1975). But as Shirley Williams has often said recently, examinations do not tell the whole story of the background of the pupils at the school. Lists of examination results would be misused by the media and would exalt some schools, who were not doing a particularly good job, in a favoured social area, while penalising those which were in a socially deprived one. We have toyed with an idea of a Value Added Test which could be appended to make the bald facts of examination successes more fair. But the complications of devising such a test make nonsense of the exercise. Until the atmosphere changes, or until some sophisticated counter-measurement can be devised, parents should be told the results only of their own children's examinations.

When we asked teachers in Lancashire what they thought of the authority's plans to introduce standardised tests, some of them said they did not mind provided they knew beforehand exactly what the tests were to be used for. In that particular case most were satisfied if they were told the tests were going to be used as a basis for distributing resources. The objectives of a national examination system should include this, but should be broadly three-fold. First, it should test children in the common core curriculum and guarantee standards in those basic subjects. Second, it should lead to a school-leaving certificate for those who are going to leave school at sixteen and go into employment or further education. Third, it should lead to higher education and guarantee standards there.

We propose a three-tier examination structure, to be run by regional examination boards. We would hope that it would be possible to confine the number of these to eight — the present number of GCE boards — but they would be split up into regions representing parts of the country like the fourteen CSE boards.

The age at which the examinations could be taken would be flexible, subject to safeguards to prevent early specialisation. The *Basic Certificate* (to be called B Level) would be taken normally at the age of 14, that is during the third year of an 11—18 secondary school. *Ordinary level*, an examination which should combine the examining system of CSE with O Level, but be called O Level, should be taken at any age but generally at the age of 16. It would be a single-subject, highly flexible examination and any part of it could be taken by adults who had left school. Normally schoolchildren would attempt five or six subjects, balanced as far as possible, but a mathematical, scientific and literary element would be compulsory. Lastly, *A Level* should be taken at 18-plus and should be somewhat similar to Scottish Highers and Sixth-Form Studies. There should be a distinction between major and minor subjects. The normal pattern would be to take two major and three minor subjects.

The new examination, B Level, is, of course, related to the common core curriculum described in Chapter 5. It would guarantee that the school fulfilled its basic obligation: to ensure that children leave school numerate, literate and possessed of certain other elementary knowledge and skills which can be adequately tested. A child who had passed this test should be seen as a relatively competent, independent member of society. To pass it, with whatever degree of special

106

help may be needed, should be regarded not only as a goal for each child, but as a *right*, freely open to all children. It follows, then, that a child who leaves school without passing the test should be able to take it later, and ideally have instruction provided free to pass it at whatever stage of life and at whatever place he wishes.

The testable core skills were identified in Chapter 5 as reading, writing, calculating, understanding the rudiments of practical mechanics and electronics, and the use of one living language other than one's own. We therefore propose an oral, written and practical examination in four main fields: literacy, numeracy, elementary science and modern languages.

Before discussing the content of these three examinations, there is a general point to be made. The certificate awarded at the successful completion of the B Level examination would be one within the power of more than 80 per cent of all children. There is growing agreement that while about 2 per cent of children are now registered as needing special education, there is in fact a far larger proportion — perhaps about 20 per cent — who at some stage or other in their school careers will need extra educational help, either because they are slow learners, or because they have specific learning difficulties, or because of behavioural, health or other problems. We envisage that a considerable number within this 20 per cent range would ultimately, given the help they need, be able to take all of the B Level except the modern language element, and many might take that too.

Preparation for B Level would occupy a proportion of the curriculum; it would not take all of it even in the case of those children who found it difficult. The other compulsory but non-examination subjects would take up the rest of their time. Normally children would have to pass B Level before going on to O Level, but children with severe reading and writing difficulties could study for O Level mathematics or practical subjects while still working with remedial help for the B Level in literacy, and there would be other exceptions, to allow those who were slow in one skill to go ahead and not be held up unduly because of it.

For some children, then, the B Level would constitute a goal, and a useful one, which would bring their education into line with the education of much quicker and cleverer children, albeit at a different pace. This does entail, and we fully recognise this, that there would be a number of children, probably 50 per cent of the ability range, for whom the B Level examination would be no sort of challenge at all.

When we discussed such a plan with representatives of the Schools Council, they said that the examination would 'mean nothing' because it would be far too easy. But this seems to us a short-sighted view. The Driving Test does not 'mean nothing' simply because for some people it is extraordinarily difficult, and for others extraordinarily easy. The Driving Test has the purpose of ensuring a minimum standard of skill. Mercifully many people have far more than this, but they are not therefore exempt from the test; they can go on and take an advanced form of it.

For the child in the top 20 per cent of the ability range, the B Level would not require much direct preparatory teaching. He would learn to express himself in learning other things, and to calculate, and to speak in French or mend a fuse. This means only that on the appointed day he would take his B Level without a great fuss, just as many children used to take their 11-plus examination, and hardly notice it. But because the skills tested in the B Level examination are useful and are tool skills, as we argued, no time need be wasted on teaching *for* the examination. The skills must be taught in teaching other things. The presence of the examination *for everyone* would, however, ensure that those who had difficulty did get extra teaching. This applies of course to pupils who are highly gifted in one field, and retarded in others, who might otherwise emerge with a parody of an education.

We envisage a considerable enlargement of remedial teaching in all schools, and therefore a considerable degree of flexibility in the withdrawal of children for some of their time from classes, in order to work specifically for B Level. Mixed-ability methods of teaching could still be used, because they do not entail mixed-ability classes for all thirty-five lessons a week. Certainly there could be mixed-ability form bases, from which children could move, according to ability, for most of their time, or only for a small part of it.

The comparatively elementary nature of the B Level examination would not hold back the more intelligent children. Since it would be principally an examination in skills without a great deal of factual content, there would not be pupils chafing at the bit to take it and get on, as there were in the early days of GCE O Level, when it was supposed not to be taken before the end of the fifth year, or the age of sixteen. Teachers would have a fair amount of choice to decide what mathematics children did, how far they went in learning a language, and the levels pursued in the other compulsory fields. There would be a good deal of freedom for schools to organise their timetable in any way they wished to up to the age of fourteen, so long as the two circles of curriculum subjects were kept up.

Any compulsory examination of this sort is likely to be criticised on the grounds that it would dominate the curriculum even in the primary school. In one sense it *should* dominate the curriculum in the primary school. We do not want only the B Level subjects to be taught, and we hope we have made this clear. On the other hand, if the teaching of the basic skills did not largely dictate the pattern of primary-school teaching, the purpose of the B Level test would be lost. The extent to which the curriculum would be dominated by the need to fulfil the country's educational obligation to the child would depend on the ability or the educational difficulties of that child.

Another criticism of the B Level is likely to be the emotionally charged one that it is a return to the 11-plus. The differences are, however, obvious.

However much schools might wish to exercise their flexibility about the age at which the test should be taken, it should not be taken at primary school. So secondly and more importantly, the B Level would not be a selection instrument to decide which type of school a child should go to. The only sense in which the test would be discriminatory is that it would reveal which children needed special help in which of the basic skills. Just as a school medical examination picks up, it is hoped, conditions which ought to be treated before worse befalls the child, so the B Level would pick out the children (if they had not already been discovered) who were still struggling. It would be an examination for positive discrimination rather than an examination for privileged schooling.

109

The other great difference between the B Level and the 11-plus is that the latter could be taken only once (except in very special circumstances when a re-try was allowed). We envisage the B test being taken again and again if necessary and in bits, skill by skill, if that is thought more suitable for a particular child.

If a national test in basic skills at the age of fourteen is thought necessary, then greater expertise than we can muster would obviously be needed and much more work should be done on defining the actual skills that should be tested.

First, literacy. We suggest that a child should be tested on his ability to read and understand a popular newspaper. The comprehension test would be partly written and partly oral and would entail no more than answering some factual questions about the content of one or two stories, features, editorials. The child would also be tested orally and in writing on another piece of narrative or descriptive but straightforward prose. He would also be required to write a letter, perhaps applying for a job or explaining that an article he had bought from a shop was faulty. He should be able to fill in simple forms and not be panic-stricken by the sight of more complicated ones.

As far as numeracy goes, the skills which should be tested are: basic addition, subtraction, multiplication, division, fractions and the use of decimals. The calculations ought to relate to those needed in everyday life such as measuring the amount of floor covering for a room or the ability to read the dials on a gas meter. Some testing on the general notion of large numbers would also be appropriate. For example, children might be given the population figures of two places, and asked how many more there are in the one than in the other. Or they might be asked how much further the sun is from the earth than New York is from London, after having been given the distances of the two sets. The basic test proposed by the Institute of Mathematics in February 1977 contained such questions as: 'John paid £2.52 for seven large tins of dog food. How much were they each?'; and 'A bedroom suite is in a sale where everything is marked 20 per cent off. The normal price is £225. What is the sale price?' Calculators should be discouraged until this part of the B Level test had been passed.

Moving now to elementary science, a term which covers a very wide application of general knowledge and practical skills, the aim would be partly practical: to ensure, for example, that a child at the age of fourteen could change a plug, mend a fuse, understand the rudiments of how the internal combustion engine works, the basics of household plumbing, what the different components of a normal diet are, and other practical uses of knowledge which would be of help to him later. The syllabus should also prove interesting enough to enquiring children to want to know more. Our purpose would be only partly fulfilled if the B Level science test did not encourage children to go further into pure science or into technology.

In modern languages, most pupils would take an oral test to show that they had some grasp of the skill of communication in a language other than their own. The kinds of skill which would be tested are those normally needed on holidays: ability to handle foreign currency and to ask the way in another language and then understand the directions given. The fact that the B Level test for a language would be the same for everyone would not involve teaching everyone up to the age of fourteen together, or by the same methods. It is absolutely essential in this field that teachers should have the skill and the authority to divide the able from the less able pupils. The DES document published on 17 March 1977 (*Modern Languages in Comprehensive Schools*) said: 'Given the wide range of ability of pupils learning a modern foreign language . . . it is most regrettable that so few modern language departments have given thought to the needs of pupils of differing abilities.'

This was one of the reaons, the DES said, for under-performance at all levels of ability. It is generally recognised that in the case of mathematics it is absolutely necessary to separate the able from the average and the average from the low-ability pupils in the matter of the actual content of the course. The same is true of modern languages. By the age of fourteen an able pupil should not only be able confidently to conduct conversation on simple topics fluently, but should be able to read to himself in simple prose. He should be able to understand a language spoken at normal speed, at least on simple topics. To do this he will inevitably need to have

111

been taught a certain amount of grammar. In our view this means that, early on in secondary schools, children will need to be put into sets according to their ability for mathematics and language work.

There will be some difficulty over the choice of a second language. Most pupils would be offered French in the first instance because of the teachers available; but German and Spanish should be actively encouraged as alternatives. Most able children should be encouraged to start a third language at least in their second year at secondary school and to do a B Level test in it as well. Immigrants with little command of English would be encouraged to do English in the language as well as in the literacy test. If teachers were available to understand them, they would be allowed to offer their own home language as a second language. This system could operate in Wales in a somewhat modified way. Children who were being taught in the Welsh medium would do their literacy test in Welsh and their modern language test in English. Welsh pupils not being taught in Welsh could offer it as their second language although they should tackle a foreign language as soon as they could.

The B Level examination, then, would be something which at least 80 if not 90 per cent of children would pass by the time they left school. For a minority it would be the only certificate they had on leaving school. But at least they would have something to show for eleven years of compulsory schooling. The nation too would be seen to be doing something about the scandal of large numbers of 16-year-olds leaving school illiterate and innumerate. The certificate would be awarded to pupils who did not pass or sit the modern language test. Normally, pupils would pass all four elements of the B test before proceeding to O Level.

The years between 14 and 16 would usually be spent on working towards this second examination. The name O Level could conveniently be kept although we entirely agree with the reasons for the Schools Council's proposal for a common system of examination at 16-plus. The details of the plan are still being considered by the Secretary of State at the time of writing.

However, the feasibility studies for the new examination system undertaken by the Schools Council's working party in

1975 were far from satisfactory. It was not clear whether a common examination syllabus or a common examination system was intended, and it did seem that the brightest children would not be sufficiently stretched, while the least able would be left at sea.

The present dual system of CSE and O Level is also unsatisfactory because CSE has not won parity of esteem with O Level in the eyes of employers and parents, and because of the inconvenience it causes teachers, pupils and parents in choosing which examination the pupil should sit. It therefore has to be changed. By not being shy about putting pupils after the age of fourteen into widely different examination courses, most of the valid objections to the Schools Council's plan could be met. Some way should be found of ensuring that the standards applied to the various courses remained comparable. This would have to be done by the Schools Council which would have to work out what were good, bad and indifferent performances in each field.

Children would now be entering a stage of schooling which would be 'adult', in which they would be largely choosing their own courses. These might involve long projects of their own, work-experience outside the school, lessons linked to further education colleges, and certainly lessons actually with adults who wished to pick up additional qualifications and would be returning temporarily to school or college. There should therefore be a very flexible system with many different routes to the attainment of a certificate. Some children would be able to offer all academic subjects at O Level, others only practical subjects. Some could offer all written papers, others project work, others a mixture of types of examination.

The only compulsory aspect of this system would be that all children would have to keep up some form of mathematics, science and a literary subject even after passing B Level until the statutory school leaving age. Those who might wish to go on to higher education would have to pass examinations in these subjects. Both the qualification for higher education and the wide difference between different methods of examining and hence between different syllabuses would demand that children should be sorted into different groups, according to intentions, according to which type of

113

examination suited them, according to whether they were practically minded, skilled with their hands or academically able. As far as possible they should have a tailor-made programme suited to their needs.

A large part of the reason why the Schools Council's suggestions got into such difficulty was that they were trying to satisfy the lobby that wanted a non-divisive curriculum as well as trying to satisfy teachers who were double-banking their pupils in both examinations as a fail-safe device. We don't want to satisfy the non-divisive lobby. Under our system pupils would decide with the help of their teachers and parents whether they were likely candidates for and wanted to go on to higher education, and to a more academic kind of O Level syllabus, which, indeed, they might start working on before they were fourteen. This could be done without narrowing their curriculum because a child would have to keep his B Level subjects (if he had not passed the test) and his other compulsory subjects at least until the age of fourteen, and thereafter he would still have to keep mathematics and science at O Level or A Level.

This scheme could provide a genuine continuity between O Level and A Level work. Dame Margaret Miles, former headmistress of Mayfield Comprehensive School, Putney, London, complained at the Birmingham regional conference that examinations of any kind at 16-plus disrupted course continuity between 14 and 17 and should be phased out. Likewise Dr Harry Judge, director of the department of educational studies at Oxford University wrote in *School is not yet dead* (Longman, 1974): 'Benign results would flow from a simple decision to . . . allow the 16-plus national examination . . . to wither away.' He went on to say that its disappearance would remove 'an unhelpful myth from secondary education, and free teachers and pupils to think more carefully about what they are in fact doing and why'.

This kind of argument, based on the premise that examinations are an inconvenience or an evil and prevent constructive teaching and learning seems wrong-headed. Examinations are a *good* and do allow, in fact encourage, pupils to think what they are doing, to select their courses, and to help their children to go through the same process when in years to come they reach a similar stage. Examina-

114

tions at the age which for many is the school leaving age are particularly good if they offer to those pupils who pass them a certificate of positive usefulness for the next part of their careers, and give them a motive to continue to turn up at school, in spite of temptations to truant. Truancy might be further cut if pupils who chose could do their O Level examinations at colleges of further education, alongside highly motivated adults.

There is no intrinsic reason why work for O Levels should be seen by pupils to be irrelevant or boring. The good motive behind the invention of the CSE was to find ways in which teachers and pupils together could work out subjects and activities which would be relevant and interesting as well as being examinable. With the same motive the 16-plus examination should be improved and streamlined. That means gearing it far more closely to the actual future needs of those pupils who would take it.

Most children would leave school with either one or two kinds of certificate. Some children in the bottom 20 or 30 per cent of the ability range would leave with only a B Level certificate, but most would leave with a second level of certificate which would record a wide variety of passes at O Level, and at A Level in a minor or a major subject. The minor subject at A Level would be at a standard between O and A Level. (We see no place for a Certificate of Extended Education.)

Thus a school-leaving certificate might have on it at one extreme, one pass at O Level; or at the other extreme, six or seven O Levels and three major and two minor A Level passes. The only restriction would be that everyone proceeding to higher education would have to have passed mathematics and science and would have to have one pass in a subject which entailed literacy at either O Level, O/A Level or A Level. There is no reason why the 'literacy' subject should be English. A pass in history or, say, classical literature would do just as well. We have suggested that a child at fourteen, if he can pass his B Level, should be able to read with some understanding and write coherently in English, and in order to pass an examination in history at O Level, or of course at A Level, he would have had to develop both these skills. It would be perfectly reasonable for

115

a history candidate's exercise of them to be taken into account by the examiner. He could not, therefore, allow them to drop after his B Level examination, and this is all that has to be ensured. We would not want to restrict the range of the subject content of the 'literacy testing' examination. There is no reason why new syllabuses, perhaps crossing borders between literature and history or history and music, or geography, should not be devised. Similarly, science subject-boundaries could be crossed. The tripartite requirement, however, should remain that mathematics, science and literacy should all be represented at least at O Level.

It is essential for the bodies who will receive pupils after school — universities, polytechnics, hospitals, professional training establishments, and employers — to lay down what they demand by way of qualifications and for examination boards to write their regulations accordingly.

Such a system would broaden the narrow two or three A Levels curriculum and bring it more into line with Scotland and countries on the Continent. A Schools Council working party has carried out a simulated exercise in N and F Levels which are similar to the A Levels we are advocating. It found that the numbers taking mathematics would increase by about half as much again, and many more would keep on languages and other minority subjects.

Under our scheme the only university faculties which would apparently have to modify their entrance requirements are the medical schools which at present insist on either three A Level sciences or two sciences and mathematics. It could be argued that a five-subject sixth-form course, even if three of the subjects were minor ones, would reduce standards of entry to higher education all round. Most modern language faculties insist on students passing two languages at A Level and they could argue that these two languages could not be so thoroughly learned as part of a broader course of five subjects instead of three. However, if language teaching were generally improved throughout the school, this argument would not be very powerful. Science (other than medical) and mathematics faculties would probably find the new system acceptable, and other faculties in the arts would have no difficulties. Many candidates for English

116

universities come up with Scottish Highers and do very well. Others study subjects successfully at university which they never studied at school, such as philosophy, psychology, even English and geography. If the various outside bodies set their own demands among the possible combinations of major and minor subjects to be studied in the sixth form, then we believe examinations at 16-plus would also fall into place.

Technically it would be possible under our system to by-pass O Level altogether. But the point of doing O Levels would be to widen experience and to render subsequent choice of specialisation more realistic and better informed.

There is considerable merit in the suggestion that pupils and adults might, if they wanted to, take external graded examinations step by step, and that these examinations should lead towards an O Level or an A Level. This is a system which everyone takes for granted in the case of music. For example, pupils can take music examinations for the Associated Examining Board from grades one to eight, in both practice and theory. There is a link between these and O and A Levels, in that a Grade V practical can form an essential part of O Level, and a Grade VII of A Level. Such a system could well be extended into other fields. Mr Michael Marland, headmaster of Woodberry Down comprehensive school, London, suggested this at the London regional conference, arguing that candidates in modern languages should work for interpreters' badges at various grades. Mr Marland said that pupils needed to know where they stood by some objective external standard as part of their emotional development. They did not want to wait until they were sixteen and a half.

Finally, whatever the details of the B, O and A Levels might be, they should be administered, set and marked by eight examination boards regionally distributed. Mode 3 (CSE) which involved a teacher in a particular school marking the work of his own pupils should be brought to an end. No school should have any right to its own peculiar syllabus. Syllabuses should be agreed by the regional board and should be available to all schools. Teachers, as well as members of universities and polytechnics, should serve on the boards, and on their subject panels.

The marking and assessment of project work, though it

might well be undertaken by serving teachers, should be done by a pool of examiners, and a teacher should be disbarred from assessing in his own school. Only in this way would the general public believe in the fairness and the uniformity of standards in the examination system.

The advantages of having eight boards are numerous. Schools get to know their own regional board and establish a good relationship with it. Teachers, who must be deeply involved in the work of the boards both as examiners and as members of subject panels and advisory committees, do not have to travel vast distances. And syllabuses particularly relevant to areas within the region can be devised.

If the system is to work it is absolutely essential that the Schools Council regain its power to validate all examination syllabuses which it relinquished in 1970. It must be its own Council for National Academic Awards and the place to which curriculum demands from the various outside bodies will be directed. It must have the duty and we hope the expertise to ensure comparability of standards throughout the country. But before describing its new role, we should first describe the role of teachers which our suggestions would entail, and the implications of that role on teacher training.

regarded as having the priority it ought to have. One must therefore get the theory, the presuppositions, the *point* of education clarified first. Then the training of teachers should follow.

Everyone agrees that teachers must in future be more carefully selected. They must be of a 'high calibre'. Examples of bad teaching, possibly unfairly, were spotlighted during the Debate by a *Panorama* programme on BBC television which showed some very difficult classes at Faraday comprehensive school, Ealing, London. Qualifications do not at present necessarily relate to performance. A few days after the BBC programme was shown, Mrs Saxon Spence, a Devonshire Labour leader, told the regional conference in Exeter: 'I was a highly qualified teacher, but one of the most incompetent. *Panorama* would have enjoyed watching some of my classes.' But to speak of 'calibre' is distressingly metaphorical and vague. Do we look for academic excellence or for a particular kind of personality? How are student teachers to be selected?

If, as seems certain, teaching is moving towards being an 'all-graduate' profession, then academic qualifications are necessary. Officially recognised teaching degrees which are of a lower level than other degrees must be avoided. Of course everyone suspects that some degrees are worth more than others; but this is not part of official doctrine. The days of the 'pass' as opposed to the 'honours' degree are almost over (except in Scotland). If teachers are to be graduates then they must graduate at a level comparable to all other degrees and nothing less should be counted as a degree. If this becomes so, then the minimum entry qualification ought to be the same as for other degrees. Under our system this would mean would-be teachers passing two major and three minor A Levels, including mathematics, science, and a literary subject at A or O Level. But even given this amount of academic competence in the candidates, how much academic content should there be in the course of training itself?

Ever since the James Report on Teacher Training in 1972 the received view has been that, ideally, teachers ought first to pursue an academic course of education, which should be followed by a professional training. This pattern is thought to ensure that the academic or subject-based part of the

120

course is kept pure, and not watered down; and also to ensure that people who embark on the course are not irrevocably committed to teaching and nothing else. The James pattern was designed to allow people who had completed the first, two-year, cycle of education to break away and complete their education without reference to teaching if they wanted to. So the James recommendations were for education in three stages: first the Dip.HE (Diploma of Higher Education) which would be taken after two years and which could be counted as two years' credit towards a degree or a three-year degree course in any subject at a university or polytechnic. Both these alternatives formed the part to be known as 'personal education'. It was supposed to be geared to develop the teacher's interests and to have nothing directly to do with his teaching. The second stage was a professional training to be undertaken in a recognised teacher-training college. The third stage was 'in-service training' when the candidate would already be a 'licensed' but not fully certificated teacher.

In some ways the James recommendations have been over-taken by events. Disastrously, the third cycle, the in-service training, upon which the James Committee laid most stress, has simply not been properly implemented. Perhaps the Great Debate and the possibility of DES intervention may at last give this recommendation more urgency. We shall see.

Also, for various reasons, the distinction between 'personal education' and 'professional training' does not look as clear-cut as it did at the time when the report was published. This is partly because the status of education as a proper subject of study at undergraduate level has risen in the last five years. It is now recognised that, at least in combination with some other study, it may well make a good undergraduate degree subject. (York University has pioneered this field.) Partly it is recognised that an increasing number of graduates will want to come into teaching, not because of a passion for French, or Latin or mathematics, but because *teaching itself* interests them. An increasing number of students who read philosophy or psychology or sociology as their first degree subject (or these subjects in conjunction with each other) are interested in teaching. Their first degree will in one sense, of course, have been 'personal education', but it will also have been such as to interest them specifically in teaching. One can

121

envisage a bit more of the theory of education being incorporated at least as an option into such degrees, and in this way the boundary between 'personal' and 'professional' education would become flexible.

Much ingenuity was expended in the James Report on trying to ensure that those who trained, or partly trained, as teachers were not thereby stuck with teaching whether they liked it or not, because they were not fitted for anything else. Another way of looking at the problem was to say that the aim was to ensure that those who started on the course would not be too disappointed or frustrated if they could not get a job in teaching. It does not seem, now, as though this is a very great problem. We are becoming much more accustomed to the idea that someone with a degree in, say, English, may take a job in some area which has nothing whatsoever to do with his degree subject. Not everyone who studies history at a university or polytechnic intends, or in any way expects, to end up as a historian. The more academically respectable education becomes as a subject, the less those who go in for it will expect necessarily to end up as teachers. It will become increasingly common to see them in journalism, publishing, the Civil Service, industry or any other field where graduates are employed. So it is not necessary to be quite so insistent as the James Committee were about separating the professional from the personal aspects of teacher education.

This does not mean that the professional elements are in any way less important than the James Committee thought. On the contrary, with the growth of comprehensive education and the widespread dissatisfaction with the actual effectiveness of what teachers are able to do, the importance of professional training is greater than ever before. All teacher-preparation should ideally take four years; and whether the first three degree years contained or did not contain an element of education in them, the fourth year should be an intensive professional training course far more directly concerned with teaching techniques than the present Postgraduate Certificate course is.

This area could be vastly developed. It would be absurd to suggest that students should spend all their time in schools during this fourth year; if for no other reason than that

122

schools would not be able to accommodate them. But far more use could be made of simulated teaching practice and of tapes and films of actual classroom scenes, which would have the advantage that they could concentrate on classroom crises and difficulties and could be played over and commented on in detail. A week's work of this intensive kind could teach a student more than he could learn in a month of teaching practice at school. Obviously practice on the site is necessary. But students ought to be given far more chance than they are to tape their own simulated lessons, play them back, criticise them and have them criticised.

Such professional education should be undertaken in an atmosphere in which people other than teachers are also being educated (and this goes for the first part — the degree part — as well). There is much to be said for teachers being professionally trained alongside engineers, social workers, chemists and any other professionals. Where such complexes of different studies have grown up, the educational element should be supported even at the expense of other, more isolated, colleges. The case of North Worcestershire college of higher education, where teachers were to be trained along with college of further education students, which is tragically to be closed because of government economies, is apposite here.

In any case, the isolated colleges will probably for the most part be closed or become part of larger institutions of higher education. This is part of the DES's rationalisation plan — the so-called minimum system of teacher education — which, it is hoped, will be fully established by the 1980s. The advantages of such a system should be that the teachers will be educated with people who will enter other professions (although where the mergers are between two geographically remote colleges of education this does not seem very realistic). Also the amount of specifically teaching-orientated education will be variable and those who have a strong bent towards teaching particular children, infants or the severely handicapped for example, will be able to get some knowledge of their chosen field by the selection of options from a large range. But within such a system there would also be a fourth year of intensive professional study for the increasing number of graduates in other non-educational

123

subjects to whom we have already referred.

Students ought to decide by their fourth year, though in practice they will probably know before this, whether they want to specialise in teaching children up to the age of fourteen or in teaching children (and adults) beyond this age. The introduction of an examination at fourteen would make this a more rational division than the present distinction between primary and secondary training, which is in any case an anomaly in any area which has middle schools. Middle schools have on the whole been unsuccessful because they have been staffed largely by primary-school-trained teachers and the ethos of middle schools has been too much that of the primary sector.

A teacher who wanted to teach at the post-14 level would have to be prepared to teach adults as well, while a teacher who specialised in the earlier group would as a matter of course have to become an expert in the teaching of at least one of the inner core curriculum subjects. Although there would be differences in the professional element of the course according to which age-range it was concerned with, there would be no need to adopt a Scottish system in which if one is qualified as a primary school teacher one may not (except in remedial classes) teach in a secondary school, and vice versa. There should be mobility between sectors as far as possible. The English practice should be retained, by which, if one is a certificated teacher, then in principle one is entitled to teach anywhere. The wider the range of ability within single schools, and the more academically respectable teaching young children, or indeed slow-learning children, becomes and the further we move towards an all-graduate profession, the more rational the English system appears.

After the fourth, fully professional, year a teacher should embark on an induction course of at least two weeks before actually starting to teach, and these courses should be run by practising teachers of experience who are well paid to run them. The final part of training should be in-service training, again based mainly on schools, or on teachers' centres, colleges and schools together. There is an inevitable tension between schools, colleges of education and local authority advisers over the question of who should run in-service courses. It seems obvious that there should be co-

124

operation at this level. In an ideal world staff at school and staff at college would be neither jealous nor snobbish about one another and would see that each had an essential contribution to make to in-service courses. Both would use the advisory services.

Tension would be eased if there was money available for such courses. This is the essential thing. In times of enforced economy, local authorities will be tempted to cut down the money they spend on in-service training and they will be extremely unwilling to second teachers to courses even where they exist. Dr Harry Judge has warned that unless the Government intervenes, in-service training will disappear within a year and 'render derisory the present stress on improving and changing teacher performance' (*New Society*, 21 October 1976).

We have no way of costing our examination proposals suggested in the previous chapter. But we hope they would lead to an eventual saving from the rationalisation of examination boards. While no more money can be looked for to increase the size of the education budget in real terms for some years, education should continue to get the same proportion of the national budget and benefit financially from savings made because of the declining numbers of schoolchildren. Such savings must not go outside the education service, otherwise the prime ministerial launching of the Great Debate will prove a sham. Much of this saving should go towards extending in-service training. Perhaps too the Government will have to earmark money for the running of in-service training. Shirley Williams has promised to look into this measure, unpopular and suspect though it would be with local authorities.

Perhaps teachers should serve a longer probationary period, and during it should undertake at least two courses of in-service training. Their salaries could be increased to their notional starting level only when these courses had been completed. A system of loans for new teachers would make this arrangement possible and not unduly harsh. In any case the present circumstances demand that those who want to go in for teaching should be at least as ready for personal sacrifice and hardship as those who go in for medicine. If the teachers are prepared to use the medical model to support

125

their professionalism and autonomy, they must also be prepared to accept it in the matter of training.

Later in a teacher's career there should be further qualifications to be gained by more courses, to be taken either by full-time secondment or, more plausibly, by part-time study, perhaps by building up separate modules to make a further degree or diploma course. In this way a teacher could, for example, begin to specialise in teaching slow learners, or the deaf, or in remedial work, or in teaching specially gifted mathematicians or musicians. Such extra qualifications should merit bigger salaries and so it would be reasonable to expect teachers in post to pay for their own in-service training since the long-term gains to themselves would be manifest. Here again loans could be made available.

Even if teachers pay their way, in-service training will inevitably be expensive, and it must be recognised that it has top priority and cannot be done cheaply. For not only will there be a need for more advisers in every local authority, but if in-service training is to be practical and at least partly school-based, there will be a need for teacher-tutors whose teaching load will have to be reduced so that they will have time to lecture and demonstrate to students, whether probationers in their own schools or visitors from outside.

Everything dealt with so far in this chapter has concerned the organisation of teacher-training. But one ought not to concentrate exclusively on that. The James Report failed to have much effect on the quality of teaching because although its terms of reference included content of teacher training its findings were limited to the structure of it. The question of what teachers should actually learn while being trained is more important. Dr William Taylor, director of the University of London Institute of Education, told the North of England Education Conference in January 1977:

Despite all the millions of words that have heated the atmosphere around discussions of teacher education, and all the ink spilled since the end of the 1960s on this subject, I do not believe that sufficient attention ... is being given to the really important questions, which are not so much about size and numbers and distribution of places . . . but about, quite simply, what kinds of skill and knowledge the future teacher needs, and how such skill and knowledge can be communicated in a way that is effective in terms of subsequent pupil learning.

If curriculum content is the most important factor in the improvement of education at school (and that has been argued in the preceding chapters), then teachers must themselves believe this and must learn to teach what is central to the curriculum. But they must learn more than this. For the Great Debate started from a growing uneasiness about teachers' powers. Teachers were thought to regard themselves as above interference, as responsible for the curriculum, and, through the Schools Council, as largely responsible for examination syllabuses and standards. Yet they seemed to be accountable to no one, and to be increasingly out of line with what society actually hoped for from its schools. The new training of teachers must bring them to a different view of themselves and of their professionalism. It must make them *more* professional, and therefore more trustworthy to the outside world. This outcome will not just come by introducing stiffer entrance requirements. Teachers must also be taught a new attitude to their own standards: they must learn to monitor their own performance, to distinguish between success and failure in a way which will be intelligible to those outside the school, and to explain the purpose and likely outcome of what they are doing. This does not mean learning more of the theory and philosophy of education. On the contrary, it means learning a great many more practical skills than most teachers usually have now at the start of their careers.

In addition, therefore, to learning techniques of teaching at least one or two of the inner core subjects (if he has chosen to teach the under-14 age groups) or of teaching his own subject speciality (if he is concerned with those over the age of 14) there must be other skills the teacher must learn.

First he should be ready to contribute to the teaching of the social studies element in the middle circle of the curriculum, and this could well involve him in using audio-visual machines, selecting material, taping programmes and so on.

127

Such skills will in any case be increasingly needed for all his teaching.

Next, and at a quite different level of skill, he will need to learn to recognise differing educational needs in his pupils. He must be taught to understand how to recognise the symptoms of educational difficulty, to observe when a child is not flourishing, and to be sufficiently confident to seek advice in such a case. He must learn enough about the common signs of trouble to be able to turn to expert advice before it is educationally too late. He must also learn to recognise a child who, for instance, will be able to take his test in the inner core subjects with no trouble and who is ready to pursue his own bent, who needs advice about what books to read, what languages to start, even what sort of career to think about, at an earlier stage than most of his contemporaries. The bright child, and this includes the ambitious and hard-working as well as the genius, should be picked up and helped just as much as the struggling or the handicapped.

To do this systematically the trainee teacher must learn how to assess what a child has actually learned. He will have to learn about techniques of testing, and also of record-keeping. He will have to learn how to devise an individual programme for a particular child which is derived from the common curriculum that all the children in his class are pursuing; and this will entail his having some grasp of what is a reasonable step to expect a child to take at a particular time on his way along the common course. He must learn something of the nature and proper structure of project work and above all of assessing such work; and he must learn, too, in as far as it can be taught, the skills of classroom management and of keeping discipline. The importance of learning more classroom management cannot be over-emphasised. In training colleges teachers must learn to tape-record their performances — real or simulated — and to have them criticised in detail for their manner, their success in defining goals and their success in achieving these goals and adapting them to different pupils' needs. Teachers must learn by this new 'micro-teaching' method (detailed analysis and evaluation) to be constantly watchful and critical of their own performances.

128

This is a formidable programme for the professional part of a student's training. But it is not too much, provided it replaces some of the more speculative aspects of philosophy, psychology and sociology which occupy too much of the programme at the moment. Some aspects of the courses would be reinforced, moreover, both in teaching practice and in the in-service component of training without which a teacher should not be fully qualified to teach. (For teachers already in post, in-service courses in some of these topics, if not all of them, should be instituted immediately.)

The new, more highly professional teacher should not be content with the haphazard methods of record-keeping or of research which at present prevail. If a teacher is to regard himself as personally involved in maintaining standards, he must also feel that his experience should be made available to other teachers, and that his judgement and discrimination could actually be used to benefit not only his pupils but the whole education system. Teachers should therefore keep records of their work with pupils. Some of these may be records of success or failure of their own innovations. If they wish to argue publicly for a new syllabus or a new method, they must be able to back up their case with recorded results. But they should also keep up a standardised form of assessment leading to a profile of each pupil.

Whether such profiles, the summaries of a standard assessment procedure, should be made available to parents is a matter of controversy. If they are to be accessible to local authorities, school governors and teachers, then it seems only reasonable that they should be accessible also to parents; that is, each parent should be able to inspect the profile of his own child. This is probably right. The danger is that it will lead to a formalisation of the profile to a degree which would render it useless, and that behind the profile there would lurk the 'true' and unrevealed estimate of the child. Such an estimate would then be referred to but only verbally by the head teacher if he was required to give his recommendations about a pupil for employment, or for placement in another school. This would be the old boy network run mad. But if the profile is a common form; if it consists, in fact, of a series of ticks in boxes, the meaning of which is well understood, then faith in its objectivity can be built up, and it can be explained both to parents and to other interested parties. There must always, however, remain some material about a child, whether factual or matters of opinion, which should be kept confidentially by the school. But this is not incompatible with the keeping of objective and open records.

Open records would have obvious research value. Moreover, they would serve as a means by which a teacher could check on success or failure. The value of standardisation in this field is obvious. All too often at present teachers are secretive. They may deeply believe that what happens in their school is good, but they are unwilling to compare it accurately with what happens in other schools. Parents, local advisers and national inspectors would all benefit from standardised records. Teachers themselves would benefit most of all. For the most important consequences of a new attitude to professional training would be a new sense of a common goal for teachers, and a new determination, therefore, to meet each other, to learn from each other and to give up time to improve education as a whole.

There is wide variation in the use of teachers' centres. They could play a more important part than they do now in the general move towards higher standards. Here the teachers should begin to accumulate the material for research in which they should play a vital part. For they are, after all, the workers in the field. It is encouraging that university departments of education are increasingly seeking the cooperation of teaching in joint research projects covering various aspects of education. The universities of Sussex and Oxford are both pioneers in this area. Joint research projects of this kind, perhaps partly financed by DES grants, are far more likely to have an impact on the actual practice of teachers in schools than is research undertaken by the Schools Council. The great advantage of a university department by long tradition is that it is genuinely independent, wherever its funds come from. There is no need for it to satisfy particular interests. Teachers become involved with such research projects not as representatives of this or that interests but simply because they are interested and expert. In this sort of atmosphere reforms can be explored, and teachers can incidentally arrive at a just appreciation of their own crucial function. Furthermore, if all these skills are to be taught to teachers, someone has to devise the course in which they are to be taught.

Dr William Taylor in his speech (quoted earlier) to the North of England Education Conference put it this way: 'What needs to be done is to design a course of training that recognises the integrity and value of many diverse sources of ideas and practices, but presents them in a way relevant to the needs of the beginning teacher, intellectually challenging, and capable of being built upon by subsequent post experience education and training.' He went on to argue that such integrated research, and the use of it in actual courses for teachers, needed time and resources in universities and polytechnics. He suggested that there should be a polytechnics and colleges council for the education of teachers to work closely with the existing Universities Council for the Education of Teachers. He recommended in addition that there should be a learned society, a professional body, for the dissemination of ideas in the field of curriculum development for student teachers.

Lecturers in institutions of teacher training need the support of common research and access to new materials. They need, in fact, something equivalent to teachers' centres. But they must also have access to the work which teachers themselves are doing in schools. If the training of teachers is to be genuinely practical, and, more important, if it is not all over again to become isolated from the actual educational needs of the pupils who are at the receiving end of the whole process, then the gap between lecturers at colleges and teachers at schools must be closed. Both lecturers and teachers must see themselves as *jointly* responsible for in-service training and for the induction and school-based teaching practice which students undertake. They must, moreover, feel themselves jointly engaged in research and in assessing classroom methods and curriculum development. Where it is geographically possible, teachers' centres should also function as centres for teacher trainers. The resource and the research materials could all be stored there. Mutual support and respect would develop more freely in an atmosphere where libraries and other resources were shared. There should be a full and genuine two-way

131

dialogue between practising teachers and lecturers. A frequent complaint during the Great Debate was that lecturers were becoming cloistered in colleges and had not been seen in a classroom for at least five years.

The teachers' centres, paradoxically so greatly admired in the United States, although under-used and misunderstood over here, should play a far greater part in both the long-term and short-term education of the teaching profession. They should be storehouses of information; they should be places where advisory teachers and college lecturers should meet; they should contain banks of approved examination questions, libraries of tape-recordings, and should, in general, supplement the resources of individual schools and colleges in an area or even in a whole region. Above all, they should be the means by which teachers can be cured of their tendency to parochialism. In addition to colleges of education, centres can be used to make in-service training a reality.

Teachers could raise their own standards in a relatively short time with the help of government funds earmarked for that use. The only remaining doubt is whether the profession as a whole wants to do so. Becoming a better, more professional, teacher takes time. Teachers work hard by day. It is sometimes very difficult to get them to do anything whatsoever after the school day is over, and this is hardly to be wondered at, at least for those who have a vast load of marking to do, and who are conscientious about doing it. Women are worse than men at taking on extra work after 4 p.m. All too often they use their husbands as an excuse. It is not unduly brutal to suggest that in future, with the need for fewer teachers, only those women who are genuinely ambitious both for themselves and for the profession as a whole should be recruited or retained in the teaching force. Women teachers, who form a greater part of the profession, should campaign not for more consideration from their schools but for changes of attitude in society so that their work should be recognised as having equal priority with that of their husbands.

Society asks a tremendous amount of its teachers. Shirley Williams told the conference of the National Union of Teachers (Easter 1977): 'To teach is one of the most

132

honourable callings known to human beings. It lays upon those who take it the heaviest and most precious of obligations.' Students who are to be trained as society's future teachers must realise exactly how heavy, precious and demanding, that calling is. The central role of professional training must be to give them the concrete means of satisfying such legitimate obligations. Those whose task it is to teach the teachers should form for themselves a professional and permanent link with universities and polytechnics so that the chain of research and of resources should not be broken.

9 Research and Development

'I don't know of any big industry that can get on without
an R and D department.'
— Lord Eccles, 3 February 1977.
'The Schools Council should be the most important
instrument for the development of the operation of the
education system. In any firm the most important part is the
research and development instrument.'
— Lord Alexander, 1 February 1977.

Soon after he became Permanent Secretary, Mr James
Hamilton, one lunchtime, put his finger on the crucial weakness of the English educational system. With the freshness of
a percipient outsider he spotted immediately that it was very
difficult, in fact impossible, for the local education authority
to have a coherent idea of what was being taught in schools
and how well it was being taught.

Chief education officers can look up to the last detail how
many pens, rulers, exercise books are ordered by each school;
they can find out the content of the school meals they serve
at lunchtime, the square meterage of a classroom, and they
have records on the teachers who teach at the schools; they
know their ages, their salaries and their previous employ-
ments. But what do they know about the content of their
teaching or its effect on the children being taught?

The Bullock Report found that everything depended
upon the diagnostic skill of the teacher. The teacher was best
placed to relate a child's reading development to his intellectual endowment, his linguistic competence and his home
background. In the last chapter we argued that teachers

134

should be trained to be their own researchers, to observe the children and to pick out those who need help. The Bullock Report continued: 'However, we are emphatic that a system of observation, recording and selective testing must have well-developed support services and in-service training of high quality.'

The in-service training must be provided in the first place by local authority advisers, in cooperation, as we argued, with colleges of education. But the advisers have another equally important function. They must make sure that the schools which have children with learning difficulties, not just in reading, but in any of the basic skills, get the help and resources they need. At a time when resources are limited, needs must be assessed and resources allocated by the local authority not according to the loudness of the voice of the head of a school, nor according to the enthusiasm of a particular head of department, but according to the actual needs of the school. Positive discrimination must be exercised not in particular designated areas but to individual schools.

Most decisions about allocating resources will be submitted first to an education committee of the local authority and then to finance and general purposes committees before a final decision is taken by the authority's full council. But the claim for the allocation will in the first place come from within the education office, either from the chief education officer himself or from a member of his administrative staff. But how often do senior education officers actually visit schools and see what is going on? Can they visit schools informally? What kind of coherent idea do they get of how well the teaching in a school is going?

Dr E. Owens, county education officer for North Yorkshire, not one of the largest authorities but a mainly rural area covering a total population of 646,000, has said that education officers were no longer able to spend time in schools as they ought to. He told the regional conference in Bradford that most of his time was taken up meeting the requirements imposed by recent legislation such as the laws on maternity leave for teachers, sex discrimination, comprehensive education, health and safety at work and with meeting the different members of unions, not just those representing the various teaching organisations but the non-teaching staff as well.

135

Local government reorganisation in 1974 reduced the number of local education authorities in England and Wales from 163 to 104, so that most became larger units. The difficulties of reorganisation have taken up a great deal of the education officers' time. Now, when many of the teaching troubles are over, local authorities are faced with the headaches of how to cut back resources, with reviewing their budgets and cutting back their estimates unceasingly; they are having to take painful decisions about which schools to close, which teachers to redeploy and, undoubtedly, as a result of the latest signals from central government, education officers will be looking at their sixth-form provision. Ask at any education office what its biggest worry is, and the reply will be: 'falling school rolls'.

Local authority advisers are the eyes and ears of the local education authority. The authority, the education officer and the education committee, will be dependent on them for information and professional advice before it makes its administrative decisions. But there is a danger in the immediate years ahead that administrative decisions in terms of teachers, other staff and resources will be all-absorbing, and information from the advisers on what is being taught, and what ought to be taught, will not be gathered.

The local education authority is responsible under the 1944 Education Act for seeing that efficient education is being carried out in schools. Of course this refers to administration — to seeing that the supplies needed by schools are there — and its officers are the principal agents for this; but it also, and of equally crucial importance, refers to the content of education as well as the supply. This is a responsibility that can be delegated to governing and managing bodies, but it cannot be given up by the local authorities. So as well as giving advice, local authority advisers and inspectors have the vital job of collecting information, and checking that efficient education is being carried out in the schools.

It could be argued that there is no need for this. Most teachers already recognise the needs of the children and do their best to see that the teaching they give meets those needs and the needs of society. It could be said, too, that without any need for formal collecting of records, or assess-

136

ments or tests, local advisers, head teachers, and local education officers already have a very shrewd idea where the weak links in the teaching profession and in the teaching process are.

It was an extreme example, but the William Tyndale junior school affair showed clearly that although the local education authority knew that all was not as it should be, and although the district inspector was concerned and advising the teachers at the school, his advice was being ignored in large measure, and the authority seemed powerless to intervene.

If there are schools where teaching, however well-intentioned, is carried out on the basis of half-baked theories and not according to a coherent programme and structure, then the advisers should have the backing at their elbow to make sure that the teaching programme is soundly based. They can do this only if they have been professional teachers themselves, preferably with recent experience of the classroom. The complaint expressed quite often at the regional conferences was that the best teachers were leaving teaching for jobs in administration. If the best teachers left teaching to join the ranks of the professional advisers then there should be less complaint, because if the advisers were recognised to be among the most talented of their kind, then they would be listened to with respect. The respect would be greater if the ranks of the advisers were not seen as an escape from the classroom; if the advisers after a spell of advising returned to teaching at a more responsible level and at a higher rate of pay, and to positions which still involved some classroom teaching. They could then provide the leadership to develop the attitudes on which the quality and success of the school so largely depend. (See HMI report, *Ten Good Schools*.)

But even though one adviser may be professionally respected above the rest, he or she will still be in the position of advising head teachers and senior teachers who regard their own professionalism still more highly. The teachers in a school know the children in that school better than any adviser will know them. If the adviser thinks that a teacher is acting in a misguided way, he must produce constructive evidence in support of a better method. This can best be

137

done on the basis of collective experience, not just his own, but on the basis of an intimate knowledge and evidence of better practice at other schools in the neighbourhood, dealing with the same difficulties, or at other schools in other parts of the country. So just as the teachers are the researchers in the front line in the school and in the class-room, so the local advisers are the second line of researchers, collecting and collating evidence.

This makes their task much less invidious. No one is trying to pretend that local authority advisers are not on the look-out for things that are going wrong. But equally and probably as importantly they are on the look-out for things that are going well. The great advantage of the British educational system is that it has given great scope to head teachers and other senior teachers to use their own initiative, to develop their own programmes of teaching, and to devise their own methods, and by so doing to build up morale in the school through the belief that they are doing something well. The great weakness of the British educational system is that these bright lights of good teaching practice are hidden so often under a bushel, because the best head teachers are often not the best publicity-seekers. It requires a watchful team of advisers to spot the practices and see that the bene-fit of their wisdom is not confined to one school or group of schools, but can be conveyed outside the school, outside the neighbourhood, and is there for reference and use by the community which after all is paying for it. Local advisers should be the dispassionate testers of whether a scheme is a freak, a publicity gimmick, or truly a success.

Another weakness of the educational system is the con-fusion caused by the break between the primary stage of education and the secondary. Secondary schools are often faced with the difficulties of accommodating largely unknown children mainly from perhaps four or five feeder primary schools. This weakness has been mentioned earlier in this book and it was another of those to be described during the Great Debate.

Who knows, then, of a scheme for easing these difficulties at Hydeburn comprehensive school, Balham, in the inner London division of Wandsworth? The school receives most of its children from three primary schools. Every year the

138

teachers in the final year of the primary school move on with their classes into the first year of the secondary school, replacing teachers who had been in the primary schools the year before and now go back there. And so the alternating relay system goes on. Is the scheme a freak? Does it raise more difficulties than it eases? It is not a publicity gimmick because it has not been widely broadcast. But if it is a success then it must have more relevance than to a few hundred eleven-year-old children in Balham.

It could be argued that schemes like these *are* known about. They are written about in educational journals, magazines and local newspapers. Their uses are usually relevant only to the local needs of that particular school or neighbourhood. Each school is working out the methods of teaching that suit it best and it would get on a great deal better without the interference of local inspectors and advisers, whose salaries and expenses are using up valuable slices of the educational budget.

It would also have to be argued that the accusation in the *Yellow Paper* that some teachers were uncritically applying informal methods of teaching was a figment of the imagination of the 'dessicated mandarins' who stay inside the 'closed walls' of the DES, as Mr Max Morris so vividly described the civil servants during one of his speeches to the NUT's annual conference in Easter week 1977.

If teaching methods are being applied critically and coherently, then there will be evidence of structure and results that the adviser can glance at or take away and store for reference, and the interference involved will be minimal. After all, the Bennett Report demonstrated (see Chapter 3) that it is not enough to classify teachers or teaching methods as 'progressive' or 'traditional'. It is far more complex than this crude dichotomy suggests. Teachers who have themselves been trained in classroom management will be far more aware than hitherto of what exactly they are doing. What is called 'micro-teaching' will become a necessary part of both initial and in-service training. It will make a teacher acutely aware of what his personal transactions are with his pupils and what is his actual success in reaching his goals with his pupils in a short and selected period of time. The methods of using films and tape recordings will make it possible for teachers to record what they are doing and for the advisers to learn in detail which methods are successful and which less successful. Thus the old crude distinction between formal and informal will be replaced by far more detailed descriptions.

The evidence that the school is meeting the needs of the community can be produced for the local authority. Unjustified criticisms of the school can be switfly and confidently countered. Lessons from the school's teaching practice can be stored in a teachers' centre for use by, or to provoke discussion among, other teachers. The adviser's time will not have been wasted and the school's time will not have been wasted.

If local authority advisers act as a professional check on what is being taught in schools, there is also a need for a check by lay people, who have not necessarily been teachers or involved in education beyond attending school themselves, to see that the schools are meeting the needs of society. This check is supplied quite rightly by the school's governing body. They have been given direct responsibility for the curriculum in a particular school. They cannot begin to carry out this responsibility unless the school has records of its objectives, of its teaching programmes, and of its results — examinations and other indications of success or failure — to which they can have access and compare with other schools in the area. Even with these records, there is still no way in which a governing body, meeting only once or twice a term, can properly be a major influence on a school's curriculum.

The Taylor Committee (on the management of schools), which had not reported at the time of writing, is likely to give parents of children at school a far greater representation on school governing bodies. This is to be welcomed but it is no substitute for parental involvement in the life of a school. Research has suggested that if parents are involved in the education of their children, then their children do better at school. If parents are to be involved, then they must have access to information about the school such as might be contained in school prospectuses which the Conservative Party (in the run-up to the October 1974 general election) rightly advocated that all schools should produce.

140

As well as access to a school's aims and philosophies, parents should know about the general content of teaching at a school. Why should this remain a secret while the sports facilities, the language laboratories, the science equipment, and opportunities to play in a concert are public? Parents should be able to get this information from governors or members of the local authority's education committee, who should try and spend time in schools during the day. School prospectuses and details about courses of study at each school should be available in public libraries and at local authority offices.

Some have suggested that the idea of parents being denied access to non-confidential information by schools is a middle-class obsession. It certainly cropped up often during the various rounds of the Great Debate. Mr Eric Midwinter told the conference in Preston of the National Consumer Council's survey which showed that three parents out of five did not think they were told enough about the choices available for their children. He himself was not able to see the results of his child's intelligence test and he is still wondering to this day why one of his children was put in the 'Blue Class' for mathematics. One parent, Mr K. M. Turner, from the London borough of Redbridge, specifically asked Miss Margaret Jackson, Under-Secretary of State at the DES, if he could attend the London regional conference at the Festival Hall, because, he said, 'it was difficult for parents to become involved in the education process'. A Devon housewife told the Exeter regional conference a few days later that she received one invitation a year to talk to her child's form teacher and the time was strictly limited to five minutes. She told the conference:

> I want to know why I am the one who has to read the Riot Act to my son when he cuts class detentions. I want to know why my son's exercise book is full of graphic doodles and pieces of badly written work are never corrected. I want to know why children are climbing over desks at the back of his classroom.

Information should be available at teachers' centres, public libraries and local authority offices about the primary and secondary schools on offer to parents, so that parents can

141

make a proper choice on the basis of which subjects are offered higher up the school.

Local authorities should run advisory services for parents on schools in the area. This becomes more important as the children become older and the choices more varied. But parents, pupils and other adults should be able to see what an authority has to offer at schools and colleges for the 14—18-year-olds. This is an age group which we hope will be joined by adults and, as described in Chapter 7, would contain a wide range of courses leading to O Levels. Because it is so wide it will be very confusing to parents and students unless there is a special local authority adviser in charge of adult education (including the 14—18 age range), bridging the gap between schools, sixth-form colleges — if there are any — and further education, and working closely with the careers advisers to coordinate schools, work-experience courses, day-release opportunities, training schemes run by firms and those run by the training services and other agencies. Such a man or woman should be the crucial link between the worlds of school and work.

There should also be a local authority adviser to span the gap between primary and secondary schools. This person should be responsible for seeing that as far as possible the provision between the two is connected. Rather than having separate advisers responsible for primary and secondary schools — thus reinforcing the divide — as some authorities have, special advisers would be better placed in charge of pre-14 and post-14 education. The adviser for pre-14 education would need to be a specialist in teaching and testing the basic skills of literacy, numeracy, elementary science and modern languages, which are the compulsory core subjects. It might be too much to expect that most advisers would be capable of mastering all four, and there would be need for a supporting team of advisers.

The special responsibility of the local authority would be to see that the middle circle of compulsory core subjects (PE, RE, aesthetics, sex education and social studies) were being taught. Local authorities should have specialist advisers in each of these fields and they would help draw up agreed syllabuses for each of these subject areas in conjunction with panels of teachers from a number of schools along

142

the lines of the present agreed religious syllabuses. The local advisers should keep a particular eye on how these areas are being taught. There would be scope for cooperation between teachers and local advisers. It would follow that in an authority where the local advisers had a considerable influence on teacher promotions, success in these fields could be justly rewarded. If, however, the local authority could not afford to or was not willing to give priority to these subjects, then central government should be able to earmark specific grants, so that there would be every inducement to follow the national line.

Not all authorities have a special adviser in charge of remedial education, although this would be an essential linchpin in our pre-14 department. Remedial education is too often regarded as something to be provided after a child reaches secondary school, but by then it is usually too late for a child who has fallen behind to catch up. Primary schools should share remedial departments – if they cannot be given one of their own – or local authorities should have pools of peripatetic remedial teachers who should be sent where the need is greatest. A high priority should be given to the in-service training of remedial teachers, otherwise the impact of the Bullock Report in the fillip that it gave to screening processes in numeracy as well as literacy in primary schools in almost every authority would be lost. The local authority adviser for remedial education should work closely with the adviser for special education so that the distinction between these two could be merged in some categories and the local authority departments for remedial and special education could be jointly backed by the educational psychologist, medical and other welfare services.

Local advisory teams differ greatly from authority to authority, in name because some are still called inspectors, but also in number and job description. The DES's background paper to the Great Debate, *Educating Our Children*, said that teams across the country varied in size from 4 to 94 and only roughly according to the size of the education authority. It said there were about 1,800 and referred to a tendency in the past few years for fewer of them to be only subject specialists. Almost all had administrative functions and many were involved in the promotion of teachers. The paper said: 'Not all formally inspect teaching, let alone schools as a whole. In many cases considerable changes of practice and attitude would be needed on all sides before local advisers could be put in a position to undertake general assessment of schools or even of specific aspects of pupil performance.'

It is exactly these changes of 'practice and attitude' which are needed (if the background paper is right) if advisers are to play their crucial part not just in the administrative development of the local education service but in curriculum development and in a national and local chain of information and research on education so that schools can really serve, and be seen to be serving, the needs of society.

Local authority advisers would therefore use the teachers' centres as research data banks, so that members of the national inspectorate (HMIs) could quickly glean information of a detailed kind about schools in an area by visiting a centre. Speed and convenience are of the essence because of the small number of HMIs: there are less than 450 of whom only about 260 are mainly engaged in the inspection of schools. Their number is not likely to be increased, yet every day a new area of research seems almost to be thrown their way. One speaker during the Great Debate in Cardiff referred to HMIs rather disparagingly as 'butterflies'. In a sense this is just what they should be: flitting about from authority to authority, over different parts of the country, gathering the results of local research in one area and suggesting where they might be applied with benefit in another.

Their activities are not, and should not be, confined to this country. They should be visiting other countries and gathering more information particularly about the educational systems in those countries which are competing with us in world markets. As was shown in Chapter 2, we have much in common, yet it is surprising how splendidly isolationist we still are. Little enough is known about Scotland's education system, let alone about those further afield. Mr Gerald Fowler, a former Labour Minister of State overseeing higher education, wrote in *The Times Higher Education Supplement* (4 February 1977): 'We are an inward-looking nation; but nowhere is that more apparent than in education policy. Even now, international discussion seems often to be regarded within the department as a necessary chore rather than an opportunity for cross-fertilization of experience and a source of innovation.' Britain has much to learn from other countries in the fields of adult education and education for the 16—19-year-olds where our record is plainly among the worst in the European Economic Community. Other countries can learn from our experiences with primary and comprehensive schools, and they seem keen to do so. But we do not seem to be so keen to learn from them in fields where they are more advanced.

HMIs should return to their formal practice of publishing their suggestions in handbooks containing the fruits of their research and experience and information about good practice which they have come across. The DES publishes an edition of *Trends* from time to time. This slips surreptitiously from the department with a caveat that the views inside are the views of the authors alone and have nothing to do with government policy. What we want is a new-style *Trends*, which is much more positive, and in which the HMIs write freely and without inhibition.

Is it in their nature to do so? Do they feel confined by the 'closed walls' of the DES? The most disturbing aspect of the *Yellow Paper* was not what it said about the teachers but what it revealed about the inspectorate. The memorandum suggested that the inspectorate should be encouraged to continue with its specific investigations into areas of the curriculum. It went on to say:

> Three important points follow from this policy: first, if the Inspectorate is to maintain the respect and confidence it has built up it may have to say things in its reports which will *not be wholly palatable* [our italics] to the Government of the day; second, it will have to be staffed to perform its functions in an efficient and adequate manner; and finally, we must find ways to make the general public [i.e. parents] as well as teachers aware of its attitudes and findings.

Since then the HMIs have published 'unpalatable' reports about the teaching of mathematics, science and modern languages in schools. But this passage suggests that at that stage they had inhibitions about publishing the results of

145

their findings if they showed up any failings in the education system. Does it mean that previous reports were made more palatable to the government of the day? The raising of the school leaving age in 1972 was supported by both main political parties. In April 1975 a DES report based on the views of the inspectorate (*The first year after RSLA*) said that the operation had made a good start and almost every school could report some degree of success.

All the evidence from talking to teachers at the time suggests a different picture of disruptive teenagers annoyed at being made to stay on at school and of widespread truancy. As regards truancy at least, these anecdotes received some support from the study, referred to earlier, by the National Children's Bureau of a wide sample of sixteen-year-olds, all those born during one week in March 1958. They were the first to have to stay on at school when the leaving age was raised. The Bureau's survey suggested that one out of twelve played truant often, and nearly half of the total of 15,000 said they had played truant at some time during the year. The HMIs' report contrasted oddly with one relating to the Scottish scene produced by their Scottish brethren. This report, produced in June 1976, said 50 per cent truancy rates were common, and that truancy and indiscipline among a minority of pupils were joined by apathy and indifference to new courses by a considerable proportion of pupils who were retained at schools. Was the DES *Report on Education No. 83* (April 1975) an example of a 'palatable report'?

This may be casting an unjust slur on HMIs. But not everyone accords them the respect and confidence that they awarded themselves in the *Yellow Paper* (see adverse criticism at the end of Chapter 1 in this book). The phraseology in that paper does not increase our confidence. There remains a suspicion that there could be pressure on the inspectorate from the DES to come up with reports that are palatable in future.

Like Caesar's wife, the inspectorate must be above suspicion. The Great Debate arose from a crisis of confidence in a service which the DES has the responsibility of running. Some of that loss of confidence is justified; some of it is misplaced. The nation needs its confidence restored by a continuing analysis of what is wrong and of what is broadly right. This analysis must be impartial and must be seen to be impartial. If it is carried out from within the DES and finds that most of the criticism of schools was based on the hysterical imagination of the media, the analysis will be regarded as whitewash. If it is carried out from within the Department and finds that most of the criticism of poor teaching in schools was justified, it will be regarded as just another 'mandarin' attack on the teachers. In neither way will confidence in the impartiality of that analysis be restored.

Her Majesty's Inspectors were appointed by the Privy Council's committee on education in the nineteenth century to inspect schools to see if they were worthy of grants from the committee. They are still formally appointed by order of the Privy Council. They are drawn from the ranks of the teaching profession and there is a rigid division between HMIs and other civil servants (with the exception of the senior chief inspector who is given deputy-secretary status). They do not go through the same selection processes or rise through the same hierarchical structures. Their base in the DES is one of convenience only.

They are not in the days of free education still inspecting state schools for grants; the last vestiges of that system are at present being phased out with the Direct Grant grammar schools. But the inspectorate's supervisory powers remain. They should be responsible for seeing that all schools are efficient and, in our terms, this means meeting the needs of society. The HMIs are the national agents for seeing that the guidelines which would be laid down by the Secretary of State for Education and Science on teaching in schools are being carried out. Like the local advisers, they are not just concerned with the administration of schools; they are concerned with the teaching inside them.

They are the central agents, too, for seeing that the research collated by the teachers in the classroom, the head teachers in the schools, and the local advisers in the local authority areas is available to the Secretary of State. In this way teachers could be seen to be influential in providing data from which informed discussion could start, and sensible decisions could be made. This should encourage them to innovate in teaching methods and to record their results.

Now, teachers will not be encouraged to supply the data

147

if all that happens is that it is collected, sifted and locked away in secret vaults in the DES from which selected memoranda critical of the teaching profession emerge. If teachers are to be researchers, the results of that research must end up in a forum which is open to the teaching profession. The forum exists. The Schools Council was set up in 1964 as a partnership of those who run the education system to promote education by carrying out research and keeping under review the curriculum, teaching methods and examinations in schools.

A much closer partnership between the inspectorate and the Schools Council would bring great benefits. Although there are three inspectors on the council's governing body (including Sheila Browne, the senior chief inspector), the great mistake after 1964 was to allow Lord Eccles's conception of the inspectorate as the main research and development unit to become divorced from Lord Alexander's conception of the Schools Council as being the most important instrument in this field.

An inspectorate that knew what was being taught in schools under our system would know to what extent Schools Council projects were being taken up by the schools. It seems incredible that only now after more than ten years of existence, and after more than £10 million has been spent on 168 projects, is the council attempting to find this out. This is an exercise that should have been kept under review all the time, and the only way of doing this is through a chain of national inspectors, local advisers and classroom teachers.

HMIs, local advisers and teachers in the forum of the Schools Council could contribute to a national research centre which could be based at the council's head offices in London. Research accounts for a minimal part of the Government's total education budget (0.16 per cent according to Professor Taylor, *Research Perspectives in Education,* Routledge & Kegan Paul, 1973). It is likely to be pruned still further rather than increased, but at least we should use this moiety in the best way possible and see that it complements the vast amount of uncoordinated research on education carried out by myriads of institutions and trusts and is related to seeing that national decisions influence teaching in the classroom and vice versa.

148

The Schools Council should be an information centre and a coordinator and initiator of research. Just as local advisers should produce information to the local authorities so that resources are allocated as scientifically and constructively as possible, so the Schools Council through the national inspectorate could make sure that national initiatives are based on better information rather than on hunch and political ideology.

The Schools Council, by coordinating research carried out in this country and other countries on specific matters which affect the curriculum, could bridge the uneasy gap between research and teaching mentioned in an important but not much publicised note at the end of the Bullock Report. It said:

> The findings of research studies are not always pertinent to the problems of teachers or of much practical value in the classroom. On the other hand, some have had considerable relevance and a great deal to offer to schools and yet have not been taken up. It is sometimes said of teachers that they ignore research findings, and of researchers that they fail to respond to the day-to-day problems of the classroom. There is clearly a pressing need for better communication and a closer understanding, and we would go so far as to say that it is more important to achieve this than to initiate yet more investigation in fields that have already been heavily researched. . . . There is much that remains to be learned; but there is much that has been learned that remains to be used.

The Bullock Report was thus further exposing the crucial weakness of our education system referred to at the beginning of this chapter. There is no systematic programme of research and testing into, for example, teaching techniques and methods. Educational decisions from central government downwards are based on hunch. We have already shown that the Bennett Report was the first attempt to test the effectiveness of the so-called progressive teaching style although Labour governments had encouraged that style since 1964. No one has yet taken the research a stage further and attempted to discover which patterns of teaching behaviour are best suited to which types of pupil. Yet there

149

must be a wealth of evidence buried away in classrooms over the country which could be amassed and referred to.

There have only been a few inconclusive attempts to test the differences between teaching children in mixed ability groups or in 'streams'. Yet according to a survey of 1,000 comprehensive schools carried out by the NFER in 1974/75 more than half the comprehensive schools in the country use mixed ability teaching for most of the curriculum for the first year of secondary school, and more than a third continue it into the second. There must again be a vast body of hitherto untapped evidence in the classroom for the success or failure of mixed ability teaching which under our scheme would percolate through the education system to the Schools Council and which would be considered by the decision makers before decisions were taken.

Another example of a case where decisions have been taken without any reference to research is that of small schools. Mrs Shirley Williams, soon after becoming Education Secretary, expressed support for the 'small school is beautiful' doctrine which had been privately preached by her predecessors. But has there been any research to show that children do in fact do better in small schools? The only evidence available to us was that produced by the International Association for the Evaluation of Educational Achievement whose survey of 258,000 pupils in 1970–71 suggested that older secondary school pupils benefited by being in large schools. Yet there could well be countless evidence that large schools are difficult to manage in tough urban areas which could be stored in teachers' centres and available for reference. Such evidence could have been used, for example, by Mr Reg Prentice in 1974 when as Secretary of State for Education and Science he wished to introduce a caveat about large schools in his circular on comprehensive education. He was dissuaded from doing so by members of the NUT not on any research evidence but because some vocal members of the union are headmasters of large comprehensives.

A further example of a case where research if stored in teachers' centres would have been useful is provided by the trend started by Mrs Williams at the beginning of 1977 to base the case for a more uniform curriculum on the increasing mobility of schoolchildren. It was only a few months later that her department hurriedly began ringing around research organisations such as the NFER and the National Children's Bureau to see if there was any evidence to show that moving home had harmful effects on a child's education.

It is said that one person in the NFER keeps a register on all the educational research being undertaken. But this exercise is carried out in a complete vacuum, and would appear to be as far removed from the decision-making process as possible. The Schools Council should step into this vacuum. It should commission research before decisions are taken. It could for example commission research on why so many adults have left school unable to read, write or calculate effectively. It could then influence national decisions and initiatives which might otherwise be taken for cheap short-term political reasons, or to satisfy a particularly powerful or vocal pressure group.

If the Schools Council is to use such research material it must be more closely linked to the main research institutions, particularly the universities and institutes of education. In general the Schools Council should extend its connexions into wider areas of education. It should absorb, for example, the Assessment of Performance Unit, which started as a one-man band and is doing important research, but which is shrouded in mystery as if it were MI 5 dabbling in state secrets instead of matters of national public concern. It is illogical that such a body should be separated from that charged with the responsibility for examinations. These must be brought together. With this added support, the Schools Council would be in a better position to resume its responsibility for ensuring comparability of examination standards between different boards.

A further extension of the powers of the Schools Council should be, in cooperation with advisers, teachers and HMIs, to commission programmes to be broadcast for schools (perhaps on a new fourth channel) by the BBC, the independent companies or other bodies. These programmes might have an important part to play in ensuring the full coverage of the compulsory curriculum. This might afford just one more instance of the integration of the Schools Council with other educational bodies. It is integration which we advocate. For a body with such wide and diverse responsibilities, the

151

title 'Schools Council' is no longer appropriate. It should be re-named the 'Education Council'.

The composition of the present Schools Council is in the process of being reviewed by one of its own working parties, to include more representatives from parent and industrial concerns. The council is looking at the representation of the teacher unions which at present provide 41 out of the 77 members of the governing council.

The basis for the governing body of our Education Council would be such as to reflect the criteria which we have laid down for the curriculum. Although teachers should have a majority, the three other sorts of members on the council should be interested parents, industrialists and those members of universities and polytechnic faculties who are responsible for admitting students.

Teachers, for their part, ought to separate their professional expertise, whether they teach in primary or secondary schools or in further education, from their membership of a union. Unions should concern themselves with salaries, conditions of service and pensions; and there is no shortage of work for them in these areas if they are to look after their members' interests in the present economic crisis.

Professionally, on the other hand, the teachers should be concerned with their service to the public. They should have a professional attitude to the curriculum through the Education Council. Since the Great Debate and the crisis of confidence leading up to it, it looks very amateurish to advocate the pluralistic *laissez-faire* role that Mr Fred Jarvis, general secretary of the NUT, said in his article in the TES (8 March 1977) that the Schools Council should retain: 'that each school should have the fullest possible measure of responsibility for its own work with its own curriculum and teaching methods based on the needs of its own pupils and evolved by its own staff.'

Teachers must, as we shall argue again in our final chapter, be selected as professionals to the governing body of our Education Council. If they are willing to reorganise their representation in this way, they will in fact exercise by far the greatest single influence over the development of the curriculum which must inevitably come.

10 Conclusions

'Eccles's secret garden needs to be opened again. Then the inherently political nature of school curricula can be judged in more understanding terms than some of its critics accord it. The trouble is that those who went into the garden in 1964 have closed the gate behind them.'
— Mrs Anne Corbett, TES, 13 July 1973.

It has been said often enough that education in this country is a partnership between central government, local government and the teachers. The Great Debate has added a fourth member to the partnership — the community. The purpose of education is to meet the needs of the community as well as the needs of the children. This means that the division of responsibility for education needs to be redefined.

The responsibility of central government is to make sure that schools are accountable to society and meet the needs both of children and of society. The 1944 Education Act said it was the duty of the Education Minister to promote the education of the people. You cannot promote the education of the people without having some say over what the content of that education is.

Someone has to take decisions about the criteria to which the curricula in schools should conform if they are to meet those needs. The Secretary of State should issue positive guidelines about what he or she believes to be right. In November 1976 the Government accepted the recommendation of the Parliamentary Expenditure Committee that the Secretary of State for Education and Science should 'encourage and participate in educational development

153

without seeking to control it'.

The Secretary of State has often previously 'encouraged and participated' but in the late 1960s it began to be believed that he was not competent to interfere in the curriculum. This attitude can be traced to the late Mr Anthony Crosland who told Professor Maurice Kogan: 'I didn't regard either myself or my officials as in the slightest degree competent to interfere with the curriculum. We're educational politicians and administrators, not professional educationists (*The Politics of Education*, Penguin Books, 1971).

His predecessor, now Lord Boyle, had no such inhibitions. 'I never hesitated to write frankly to an MP when I felt that a school was acting unreasonably over a matter of curriculum, even though I knew this was strictly outside the Minister's legal powers and responsibilities' (The First Alfred G. Mays Memorial Lecture, University of Birmingham, 7 May 1976). Lord Boyle also said: 'The Education Acts, and the regulation: made under them, constitute a kind of rule book for the conduct of the national education service, assigning specific rights and duties and powers to those responsible. Yet the Secretary of State has in addition the function of being a sort of ultimate referee, and he must be allowed a certain amount of latitude over when it is right for him to intervene.'

The Secretary of State should intervene now to restore a sense of direction to teaching in schools which is so badly lacking. She should issue positive guidelines as to how teaching in schools can meet the needs of society and of the children. She must encourage the adoption of those guidelines by whatever legal means are at her disposal: first by altering the examination system to meet the needs of those guidelines, secondly by the use of specific grants to encourage the teaching of compulsory subjects, and thirdly by the use, guidance and encouragement of the national inspectorate and local advisers.

There is no question of the Secretary of State imposing the guidelines by law. The beautiful ambiguity of the 1944 Education Act is a healthy way of preventing that. If the Secretary of State acts unreasonably, she is answerable to the law and can be challenged. If she intervenes in the curriculum she has no legal leg to stand on.

154

Mr Crosland believed that neither he nor his civil servants were competent to interfere in the curriculum because they were not professional educationists. But the Secretary of State has access to a highly professionally trained body of educationists — Her Majesty's Inspectors. They would be mainly responsible for drawing up the guidelines. They would be taken out of the Department of Education and Science and based independently. As was argued in the last chapter, part of their business is to assess the education service. They are in a sense judges of what is happening in schools and of what has gone wrong with the system and how it can be put right. They must be free to apportion blame wherever they wish to without inhibitions. Just as Her Majesty's Judges were once emissaries of the Crown and had to have their decisions ratified by the monarch, and are now an independent body of people, so should Her Majesty's Inspectors be seen to be free, impartial and independent. They should be based outside the DES. They should be the link between the administrative arm of the education service and the curricular arm. The DES asked in the *Yellow Paper* that they should be given a lead by the Prime Minister and other ministers to intervene in the curriculum. They were not given it, and rightly so. They are civil servants. They are the supposed experts in planning, but not experts in curriculum.

Taken out of the department, the inspectorate would be freer to work with the Schools Council, which we would call the Education Council. It would consist of teachers, local advisers and others who are experts on curriculum matters, such as examiners. The Education Council should reconstitute itself to ensure that it has expert committees on how education can meet the needs of employers and higher education as well as its other expert committees on teaching programmes and examinations.

A newly formed Education Council is the most important of our recommendations and the one on which all the others depend. In Chapter 1 we argued that education after the Great Debate could never be the same again, and that the pluralistic concept of the Schools Council had to be changed. In Chapter 2 we said the time was ripe for teachers in this country to play their part in a more centralised and rational-

ised education system, a part for which they are more
suited by temperament and training than teachers in other
countries. This is their last chance. Through a newly-
constituted Education Council, the teaching profession
must do what it should have been doing all these years. It
should be devising a coherent curriculum plan for the whole
country and it should play the principal part in monitoring,
assessing and updating that plan.

The Education Council must be an independent body with
a built-in majority of serving teachers. Only so will its
decisions be accepted by the teaching profession. The lay
and other non-teaching elements must be less than half the
total.

Lord Eccles said of the Schools Council: 'It has all the
faults of a body of people onto which people are put because
they represented somebody or other. You cannot get policy
made by people who are always looking over their shoulders
to see what the people they represent would think.'

This has been the weakness of the Schools Council, and
if the Education Council is to put itself in order, the members
of its governing body must be teachers elected for their
professional expertise rather than for their positions in any
union. A means of electing teacher-members will have to be
devised, probably on a regional basis, and perhaps through
the agency of the Regional Examination Boards. No one
should be a member of the governing body for more than
five years. Only so will there be a flow of fresh ideas, and
a critical check on the assumptions and the priorities of the
Council. The principle of turnover of membership which
applies to the governorship of the BBC and the IBA and many
other such bodies should apply equally to the Education
Council. If members were elected on this basis the non-
teaching element could be smaller. A parallel might be the
decision of the Press Council, the body which deals with
complaints against newspapers, to admit lay members in
1963. They were admitted on a 20 per cent basis, large
enough to be a significant *bloc*, to resign *en masse* if they
disagreed with a major decision, but not large enough to
polarise the council into professional and lay divisions. Its
decisions are largely accepted by the journalist profession,
and published by the newspapers concerned. Parents then

would be chosen to serve on the governing body of the council if they were interested and prepared to spend gruelling hours sitting at full meetings rather than as representatives of such parent organisations as CASE (Confederation for the Advancement of State Education) or NEA (National Education Association). Industrialists should be chosen on the same basis, but would also be members of specialist panels.

Such a body would be well placed, particularly if it was also a research and development unit as described in the last chapter, to advise the Secretary of State on the guidelines for curriculum development. These would be drawn up by the members of the inspectorate, local advisers and teachers seconded to its ranks and presented for approval by the full council before being submitted to the Secretary of State.

These guidelines should be issued as positive recommendations as to the means of achieving the publicly announced aims of education, enunciated by the Secretary of State. They should lay down which subjects are to be taught in all schools and examined externally, and which should be taught though not examined. We are in fact asking the Secretary of State to do for the nation what a headmaster should do for his school — to state clearly and publicly what his objectives are, and to specify the ways of meeting them, with perhaps an order of priority. The guidelines through the public meeting of the full council could be debated in the full glare of publicity so that the secret garden would by now be well and truly under spotlight. Any member of the public, or any organisation, would be encouraged to send their proposals for the development of the curriculum for consideration by a committee of the council.

It is in the hope that such an Education Council will emerge, and such a committee will be set up, that we two interested members of the public summarise the recommendations that have been the basis of the book:

1. Education should meet the needs both of the child and of society.
2. This implies a common element in school curricula.
3. There should be an inner core of compulsory subjects which are examinable: literacy, numeracy, elementary science, and, for most children, a modern language.

157

4. There should be a middle circle of compulsory subjects which are not examinable: physical education, religious education, aesthetics (art, music and literature) and a course called 'Social Studies'. Local advisers should check whether these subjects are being taught up to the age of fourteen.

5. The first public examination should normally be taken at the age of fourteen. It should be taken by all children and would lead to a Basic School Leaving Certificate. The examination, to be called B Level, would consist of practical, oral and/or written tests in the four inner core subjects. The Certificate would be awarded to pupils who did not pass the modern language test but passed the three others.

6. A second public examination would normally be taken by pupils aged sixteen who had passed all four B Level subjects. It would be called O Level and would be an amalgam of the present O Level and CSE. It would be highly flexible and would consist of a variety of approaches, assessment and examination techniques. Employers would be encouraged to help design the syllabuses. O Level could be taken at an advanced stage (O/A Level) which would count as one of the qualifications for higher education.

7. A third public examination would be called A Level and would be a qualifying examination for higher education. It would normally consist of two subjects taken at major level and three subjects taken at minor level (or O/A Level).

8. Those wishing to go into higher education (including teaching) would have to pass examinations in science, mathematics, and a literary subject (such as English literature, history or classical literature) at either O or A Level. These subjects would be compulsory for all children up to the statutory school leaving age.

9. Specific entry qualifications should be laid down by institutes of higher education in terms of A Level requirements.

10. Four-year teacher-training courses should include one year of intensive professional training. Two-week induction courses should be compulsory. In-service

training should be undertaken during the probationary period, after which full professional salary should be payable. Further in-service training should lead to extra qualifications. Teachers would also be trained to be their own researchers, and to keep a largely standardised form of profile on children. These profiles would be available to the local education authority.

11. Schools would be asked to publish prospectuses, including their aims and objectives, which would be available in teacher centres, local authority offices and public libraries.

12. Local authority advisers would be responsible for collecting details about teaching programmes in schools which would be kept in teacher centres.

13. They would work closely with members of Her Majesty's Inspectorate to see that examples of good practice were disseminated more widely and passed on to a central Research and Development Unit.

14. HMIs would be taken out of the Department of Education and Science and based as an independent body so that they would be free to assess the curriculum and the administrative sides of the education service. In these connexions they would work closely with the Department of Education and Science and the Schools Council.

15. The Schools Council would be renamed the Education Council to show that it was representing all sectors of education. It would have expert committees on how education could meet the needs of industry and higher education.

16. Membership of its governing council would reflect all those elements in society to whom the teaching profession is accountable: parents, employers, and higher education. Both lay and teaching members would be elected by the Council according to their interest and expertise, not according to the organisations they represent. There should always be a majority of teachers. Membership should be for five years only.

17. The council would advise the Secretary of State on

curriculum matters and would be backed by a central research and development unit.

18. It would also advise the Secretary of State on examinations and would be in charge of validating the examinations set by eight regional examination boards. It would run the centres in which these boards were based. It would run the Assessment of Performance Unit which would be taken out of the DES.

19. It would submit the guidelines for curriculum development agreed after public debate for approval by the Secretary of State.

20. The statutory religious clauses would be removed from the 1944 Education Act and the responsibility for religious education would be given to the local education authority which has the responsibility for the curriculum as a whole.